What Others are Saying about
The Changing Behavior Book!

" ... I never thought I'd say this, but I can't wait for the school year to start so I can begin using the ideas from *The Changing Behavior Book!*"

Cathy Dobbs, Vice Principal, Horizon Christian Academy
San Diego, California

"Dr. Sutton's programs were so successful we offered his training all over the country, coast-to-coast. *The Changing Behavior Book* is like having your own reserved seat right there in the front row!"

Wayne Babchuk, PhD, The University of Nebraska-Lincoln

"I tried the simple four-step process in Chapter Twenty-two, and the results blew me away! EVERY parent needs this book.

R.B., a mom (name withheld for child's sake)
Lewiston, Idaho

"Not even half-way through the book, I had already applied ideas from *The Changing Behavior Book* in several therapy sessions!"

Kurt Volz, Therapist, OSF-Holy Family Clinic
Monmouth, Illinois

"Dr. Sutton hits the nail on the head when he suggests that we cannot change others without first changing ourselves, and that people (certainly including our children) respond best to being led rather than shoved. I certainly endorse this valuable piece of work."

Tom Ziglar, CEO, and proud son of **Zig Ziglar**
Ziglar, Inc., Plano, Texas

" ... This book will change countless lives for the better."

Jeffrey Bernstein, PhD, Psychologist
Author, *10 Days to a Less Defiant Child*

"Weaving together his rich experiences with difficult children, Dr. Sutton has written a really different approach to changing the disordered behavior of children and teens, thus improving their lives and all their relationships."

George M. Roper, Licensed Professional Counselor and CEO
Valley Counseling Centers, Inc., Edinburgh, Texas

The

Changing

Behavior

Book

A Fresh Approach to the Difficult Child

James Sutton, EdD

foreword by Dr. Doug Riley

Friendly Oaks Publications
Pleasanton, Texas

*The Changing
Behavior Book*

by James Sutton, EdD

published and distributed by:

Friendly Oaks Publications
PO Box 662
Pleasanton, TX 78064
830.569.3586
fax: 830.281.2617
email: sales@friendlyoakspublications.com
Website: www.friendlyoakspublications.com
Book's website: www.thechangingbehaviorbook.com

All rights reserved

Library of Congress Control Number: 2011933812

International Standard Book Number: 978-1-878878-77-9
$23.95 USD (trade paperback)

To Bobbie,

with all my respect and devotion.

You've seen me at my best;
you've loved me through the rest.

Young people don't create the weather of strained relationships in this often difficult world. Their behavior simply reflects it. How absurd would it be to blame a heat wave or an ice storm on the thermometer?

James Sutton

Table of Contents

Foreword

What a pleasure it is for me to be able to introduce you to a new book by my colleague Dr. James Sutton. If you have read any of his previous books, or have attended his training, you already know what to expect in *The Changing Behavior Book: A Fresh Approach to the Difficult Child*. As is typical in a Dr. Sutton book, you will get a thorough review of what other writers on the topic are thinking. What's more, Dr. Sutton has a way of pulling together a diverse body of theory and research, explaining it all in a way that leaves you saying, "Aha! So *that's* why these kids act the way they do!" Then, after he leads you through the underlying causes of troublesome behavior in the home or classroom, Jim gives you clear-headed, practical direction on how to manage the situation.

As is his way, Jim does not bother with the type of advice that necessitates having a research lab or a hospital staff of twenty; rather he offers common-sense ideas and suggestions that a thoughtful parent, teacher, or therapist can implement immediately. That is precisely what we have come to expect from Jim Sutton, and it is precisely what he delivers in this his latest work.

The book starts with a simple enough question: *What is bad behavior, anyway?* If you think you can answer this question by simply describing something objectionable a difficult child might do, let me ask you to put surface explanations aside and instead go deeper into the child's world. Dr. Sutton will explain to you how some behaviors are the end result of *desperation*. That's right, desperation.

The concept of desperate behavior is a monumental step away from much of today's prevailing theory, one that contends children act in negative ways because they have yet to independently develop or be taught the skills that help them handle life's stressors effectively. While a lack of skills can certainly be a major factor behind "bad" behavior (and it *is* addressed in this book), it is also true that children who know better will sometimes act badly, and they will do so whenever they feel cornered or threatened. It is this loss of sense of safety, not necessarily a lack of skills, that creates desperate behavior. Dr. Sutton suggests we must help these children feel safe again if we want behaviors to improve.

Be prepared to take a hard look at yourself as you read. Dr. Sutton counsels, "… I cannot recall a single instance where placing blame created any positive change at all." His viewpoint is deeply child-centered, the message being that any of us who interact with children on a steady basis must learn to see the world through a youngster's eyes. Jim makes us aware of how intensely worried and frightened a "bad-acting" child might feel, bringing us to an awareness that not all negative behavior is due to negative intentions. Wouldn't that change the way we intervene?

The beauty of *The Changing Behavior Book* is that we really get two for one: Not only do we learn about causes of difficult behavior in children and how to help them change, we also learn how to change *ourselves* in ways that make us better professionals and parents.

After you read this excellent book, why not pass it on to a friend?

Douglas A. Riley, EdD
Yorktown, Virginia
July, 2011

(Editor's Note: Dr. Riley is the author of several books, including the bestseller, *The Defiant Child: A Parent's Guide to Oppositional Defiant Disorder.*)

My early thoughts on changing the behavior of difficult children centered way too much on the youngsters themselves. "It's *their* behavior," I would say. "*They* need to fix it." I advocated laying out and applying consequences until a youngster "saw the light" and changed.

A Problem With the Light

That approach worked with some, of course, but what about the youngster who *didn't* see the light? What do we do with that child? What if the bulb had burned out and there was no light to see? Darkness wouldn't provide much direction.

Piling on yet more consequences didn't always solve the problem, either. Most experts now suggest that poor behavior is the result of poor skills. It's hard to argue with that. With few exceptions, most youngsters don't care to heap trouble upon themselves deliberately.

Bottom line: Consequences don't necessarily impart the improved behavior and skills we seek. Oh, we can rub two consequences together and create quite a lot of heat (and I did), but the light that brings willful compliance can pass us by.

Scrambling for Bullets

Whether we attempt to manage a youngster's behavior with consequences or rewards, there's always been a "magic bullet" quality to the challenge. If we could but come up with the *right* magic bullet, all the problems would vanish, or that's the way it seemed.

If we only had enough of those special bullets, some super powerful interventions, doesn't it make sense we could change just about *any* behavior? There's no doubt we could accomplish much but, if we stopped there, something important would *still* be missing.

The Half Door to Healing

One of the most powerful stories of defiant behavior being erased completely involved the famous racehorse, Seabiscuit. Proof of the horse catching a glimpse of the light of opportunity and change is tucked inside a few words from Laura Hillenbrand's book, *Seabiscuit* (Hillenbrand, 2001).

> When he heard Pollard's deep voice coming down the shed row, he would poke his head over the half door to greet him.

Seabiscuit heard his jockey's voice and went to find him. Consider the impact of that. Did the horse come to the half door because he knew it would get him a star from Pollard for his behavior chart? Did he come to the door because he knew he'd be whipped if he didn't? I don't think so. Seabiscuit came to Pollard without being called because he *wanted* to.

Seabiscuit's transformation took him from a horse that would tear up his stall, bite his handlers, and refuse to run to the animal that would later defeat the seemingly invincible War Admiral in the most famous match race ever between two thoroughbreds.

I would call that *substantial* behavioral change.

The changes in Seabiscuit's behavior and accomplishments first happened not in the horse, but in the new trainer, Tom Smith, and the new jockey, Red Pollard. (That's important; they changed, *then* the horse changed.) Their approach was as simple as it was effective: Never again would coercion be used to train this animal. Seabiscuit affirmed the changes they made many times over on the track and off. And the rest, as they say, is history.

Kids Aren't Horses, But ...

Young people are exponentially more complex than horses. The demands they face every day are overwhelming. After all, all Seabiscuit had to do was run.

I won't argue the fact there are some incredibly difficult young people out there, but we can learn a few things from the Seabiscuit story. It's a fact that difficult youngsters respond better to a noncoercive approach to redirection of behavior, especially when that approach is strongly rooted in relationships that work. It is my pleasure to utilize the pages of this book to share my thoughts and experiences on growing and implementing noncoercive intervention.

Different in Two Ways

Never before has it taken me four years to write one book. I don't exactly know why this is so, but, from the beginning, I felt this book should be different in at least a couple of ways.

Change of focus: One of the two differences has been noted in the description of Smith and Pollard's success with Seabiscuit: a focus on the source of intervention, *then* the object of it. The results more than validate the approach. Of course, such a focus requires a healthy amount of insight, vulnerability and, yes, humility.

Perhaps I'm saying it took me four years to get humble enough to write *The Changing Behavior Book*. If so, I am better for it. If not, perhaps humility is a work-in-progress, anyway.

For certain, Dr. Kenneth Wenning, through his book, *Winning Cooperation from Your Child* (Wenning, 1999), jump-started my thinking on how the anger, frustration, and indifference of the adults can profoundly handicap attempts at intervention with young people. Then, of course, there was (for me) the crown jewel of all insights: psychologist Dr. Hew Len's amazing story. When he decided to work on himself first, amazing things happened in extremely difficult individuals (Vitale & Hew Len, 2007). We'll look at his story as we consider how to apply it in our work with children and adolescents.

Asking the question, again and again: The other primary difference with this book is the question that is asked at the end of each chapter: "What Needs to Happen?" The question, and the answers, are intended to stimulate thoughts and actions on how to apply the material covered in every chapter. In essence, it's a call to action, with a few ideas on what that action might be.

May we all be better bearers of light as we show young people the paths that will work for them. If we can do that, we will have accomplished much.

--JDS, 2011

Part One

Wanted: Change

What is "Bad" Behavior, Anyway?

Desperate Behavior

Why Difficult Behavior Doesn't Change

The Victim Game

Anger: Racing Fuel for Conflict

The "Loop"

Chapter One

What is "Bad" Behavior, Anyway?

The elements that make bad behavior bad exist mostly in our interpretation of the behavior. In some cases it might be more accurate to describe inappropriate behavior of children as being even "desperate."

Desperate people engage in desperate behavior. Not all children or their behaviors are desperate, but the numbers are *not* slacking off.

Dr. Marvin Marshall, author of the excellent book, *Discipline without Stress, Punishment or Rewards* (Marshall, 2001), suggests there are two reasons why children and adolescents act out:

1. They are angry and miserable.

2. Their behaviors are their attempt to "fix" the problem.

The behavioral efforts of these youngsters to fix the problem and settle issues can be so inappropriate the adults in their lives become quite upset with them. These adults are often extreme in their reaction to the child's behavior. There are two reasons:

1. They are angry and miserable.

2. Their behaviors are their attempt to "fix" the problem.

Hmm, does there seem to be a pattern here? Why is everyone trying to *fix* the problem, yet the problem often gets worse? What's happening?

When you get right down to it, adults bring more clout to the table than children, so the sides in this conflict are rarely equal. Educators and parents, even when they intend well, have the capacity to whip a conflict into a fury. It can be a guaranteed recipe for a perfect storm. Can you identify? I can.

Pager Pop

One of my first clients in private practice was a 13-year-old boy. He wasn't really all that bad in terms of the severity of whatever he was doing. He was mostly in trouble for what he *didn't* do. The boy's father would get into screaming matches with him on a regular basis. Dad would get upset, then he would call my pocket pager (some of you might remember the pager days) *constantly* day and night.

Look closely; this young man was being reinforced for defiant behavior. All he had to do was *not* do something, and Dad would launch into his performance of tirades. This whole floor show was scripted. There was desperate behavior going on all right, but not with the 13-year-old.

Dad was a setup, and he didn't even know it. In the meantime, his reactions to his son guaranteed the trouble would take up residence in his home and in his head.

Paul the Principal

In a former career I was a school psychologist. One day we were wrapping up a Special Education meeting on a high school student. Paul, the principal (not his real name), asked me to stay behind. He had something he wanted to show me.

Paul closed the door and walked over to a credenza on the other side of the room. He opened a drawer and removed some plain-paper photos of five students in the high school, all boys. Every photo had a large circle drawn around the student's head, with heavy vertical and horizontal crosshairs drawn inside the circle. Paul called them his "targets," noting he would stop at nothing to kick all of them out of his high school, one way or another.

He selected a photo from the stack.

"This one checked out this morning." With the glee of a four-year-old, Paul took a black marker and put a heavy "X" over each eye in the photo. He then shifted the page to the bottom of the stack.

"Only four more to go," he exclaimed, proudly holding up four fingers as he put his hit list back into the credenza.

That's how Paul fixed problems in his school; he threw them out the front door. Problems steadily worsened, and he began to deteriorate physically. He ultimately retired a sick, miserable man.

Paul was a magnet for problems.

Demon Child

I had a chance to work briefly with a young adolescent who had lost his mother to cancer. (That right there is enough of a load for any youngster to bear.) His problems compounded as his father eventually opened another relationship.

This boy and that woman did *not* get along. She was de
as being tough and mean; she called the boy, "Demon Child.
of the time he was confined to his room.

The father's sister and her husband witnessed the problems
first-hand during a visit. It was more than they could bear. They
offered to take the nephew home with them, enroll him in school,
and provide a bit of relief for everyone.

I saw him after they brought him home. He *wasn't* a demon
child. He was a kid who was hurting on top of enough hurt to shut
any of us down permanently. He was grateful for being rescued
(and so was his father). The boy still had plenty of issues to work
through. It took time, understanding, and patience to accomplish
stability and the early stages of healing. It wasn't smooth sailing
with the aunt and uncle, either, but at least the lad had a fair chance.

He was one of the lucky ones.

What Needs to Happen?

We all have opportunity to learn from our mistakes *if* we can
see them. But that's precisely the problem: We often don't see
them.

In each of these three little scenarios, the adults involved acted
in ways that did not solve the problems they faced. There was no
"fix" in their fix. All three needed a better plan, a more effective
and less stressful approach to the behaviors of the youngsters.

(But doesn't this describe *all* of us at some time or other in
our interactions with children and teens? Intervention powered
by frustration rarely solves the issue.)

Pager Pop: I believe Pager Pop loved his son; I really do. He just couldn't *live* with him. They were both engaged in a dysfunctional "dance" that kept Dad upset and the boy waffling somewhere between wanting to please his father and delighting in how easily he could set him off. Dad had great difficulty ever seeing how his rage and anger played into creating more of what he *didn't* want.

Like many adults, Pager Pop would need to learn to control himself as his first effective intervention.

Paul the Principal: Paul did have legitimate issues with the boys he targeted. His rigid view of his authority and how he was going to administer it, however, caused him trouble on a number of fronts, and not just with students.

Paul's rigidity caused him to fill his discipline tool box with hammers only. As a result, he saw *every* problem as a nail. If he couldn't pound these boys into shape, then he would keep pounding until they left his school. He was quite proud of how he handled these young men, while his reputation and his health withered.

Paul needed a few more tools in his box, and some ideas on how to use them.

Demon Child: Doesn't your heart go out to the boy who, in addition to dealing with the loss of his mother, had to get along somehow with his father's new girlfriend?

In all fairness, I never met this woman who reportedly was so mean to the youngster. I understand her life hadn't been smooth sailing, either. Then there was Dad, still rocking and reeling from one of the most devastating losses a person can experience: the death of a spouse.

But the boy was hurting, also. I'm certain it was reflected in his behaviors at home and school. I do know he was failing his classes.

Young people don't create the weather of strained relationships in this often difficult world. Their behavior simply reflects it. How absurd would it be to blame a heat wave or an ice storm on the thermometer?

Smashing the thermometer will not make bad weather go away. Nor would actions that further erode this boy's capacity to function create the sort of changes everyone, including the boy himself, *really* want to see.

Everyone, the boy, the father, and the girlfriend, needed a better plan and some emotional space in which to use it.

Notice that, in each instance of Pager Pop, Paul the Principal, and Demon Child, the immediate need for change was *not* in the behavior of the youngster. Hold that thought.

Chapter Two

Desperate Behavior

I wish I had heard of "desperate behavior" early on in my career. It could have saved me a few trips down some blind alleys. You've probably been there, also, if you've ever attempted to get an explanation from a youngster regarding a never-to-be-done behavior.

I've collected quite a pile of excuses and explanations from youngsters over the years, but the most interesting ones sounded something like this: "I *had* to do it, sir." (There's also another version, generally accompanied by a roll of the shoulders: "I don't know, and what difference would it make if I did?")

"No, you didn't *have* to do it!" That was my stock response, and I meant it. I now realize I often was wrong. I now believe young people (and adults, also) are sometimes driven to act out in their attempt to remain physically and emotionally alive and viable. I've come to call it "desperate behavior" because desperation is the driving characteristic.

Desperate behavior is relatively rare, but it is gut-wrenching for the person caught up in it. (If the child or teen you're thinking of has not yet reached the "desperate" phase, that's good. Interventions covered in these chapters can help assure desperate behavior does *not* occur.)

Cabin Fever

Imagine you've built a beautiful little log cabin in the woods. It's perfect. There's a cozy fireplace, a bedroom loft, and even a safe and secure basement with a sturdy ladder going down into it.

It's a perfect life alright ... until a pack of hungry wolves dis-cover there is fresh meat in the area: *you*! They decide to invite themselves to dinner. In a snarling, terrifying pack they send you scrambling for the basement.

You're safe ... for now, locked down in survival mode. The mes-sage could not be any clearer: Do whatever you have to do to stay alive. In this moment, not much of anything else matters.

But it's hard to ponder, difficult to plan, and impossible to sort out what you're going to do with all that growling, slobbering, and clawing going on just inches above your head. You're fright-ened out of your wits as your thoughts race in pictures.

And the pictures *aren't* good ones.

As if you don't have enough troubles, you notice the floor of the basement is wet: Water is seeping in. You now have wolves above you and a basement that is flooding. You will have to *do* something.

Stuck in Bad Pictures

Indeed, there are youngsters who attempt to deal with a diffi-cult world and an emotional basement that is flooding. Although it doesn't *look* like they're scared stiff and standing in a wet base-ment, their behavior says otherwise.

Desperate behavior occurs in only about one to three percent of our young people, but it counts for almost 100% of the sort of behavioral problems that don't respond to traditional discipline and interventions. They don't go away.

The problem behaviors don't go away because the youngster is in a survival mode, prompted by all those images of what will happen if he doesn't act immediately. Whatever the behavior turns out to be, it's driven by desperation, and it's almost always the *wrong* behavior.

What sort of behaviors are we talking about? They could include most any kind of panic behavior, such as extreme reaction to frustration, striking out against others, running away, or saying or doing strange things at inappropriate times.

You can try asking the child to explain to you what he's thinking, but good luck on that one. He's stuck in the images as the pictures, bad ones, move through his consciousness much too rapidly for him to describe.

Dr. Win Wenger (Wenger & Poe, 1995), originator of the concept of Image Streaming, suggests that images operate approximately ten million times quicker than word-based language. (Dr. Wenger is referencing picture-based thinking that accounts for high levels of creativity, but I believe the concept also applies to lightning-fast behaviors of survival. Things move quickly because they *must*.)

It's no wonder we have a hard time communicating with youngsters caught up in desperate behavior. We simply can't keep up with them.

What We Know

Here's what we know about Desperate Behavior:

1. *It is brought on by elements that are intrusive and frightening.* In other words, it comes on uninvited. Flashbacks, called flash memories, of past trauma are examples. They can occur spontaneously, completely on their own, or they can be triggered by people, places, things, or circumstances. Especially tough are those flash memories that cause youngsters to actively reexperience, and continue to reexperi-

ence, past trauma. Their behavior can be seen as an attempt to dislodge the images and make them go away. In effect, they're trying to *stop* the pictures.

The death of a loved one can bring on intrusive thought. I had one young patient whose grandfather had died. A week or so later, the boy saw Grandpa walk into his classroom, step up to his desk, and speak to him. The boy began carrying on a conversation with someone who *wasn't* there! Although the boy's behavior might not have scored highly in terms of desperation, his conversation with a dead man didn't sit well with his classmates. His teacher reported they began moving their desks away from his.

Not all intrusive thought is negative. One evening while doing training at the University of Missouri, I walked across the street from the hotel to check out the Columbia Mall. I stepped into a hobby shop and went immediately to the model airplane section.

Someone close to me took the cap off a can of model airplane fuel. Instantly, my mind went retro, about 40 years or so retro. The smell of that fuel took me to another place, another time …

Dad and I are building a Ringmaster Junior on the kitchen table. I see everything vividly, right down to the cut in one of the chairs of the chrome dinette set where my sister had dropped a butcher knife. I see the time on the old kitchen clock, and there's Lady, our dog. Mostly though, I'm with my father as we work on that red and white model airplane.

Those pictures were so warm and positive I wanted to take a can of that fuel back to my hotel room. I didn't, but I thought about it.

But what if the smell of that fuel had connected with some really *bad* flash memories? What if they were memories of abuse, for instance? At the very least, I would have been out of that hobby shop in a hurry. Desperate behavior can be, and often is, associated with a need to escape.

2. *Desperate behavior is driven from the deepest parts of self; it's difficult for a child to explain.* If the behavior is survival-based, it's not open to nego-tiation or discussion. It *can't* be explained.

Asking the "why" question here would be a grand ex-ercise in futility. Kindergarten teachers often see the deer-in-the-headlights look on faces of children who have never been around more than one or two other kids before in their entire lives. When they have trouble with people being too close to them, they hit them, spit on them, or do something that creates more "comfortable" space around them. In the meantime, they're in *big* trouble.

3. *Desperate behavior seeks to obtain immediate relief.* In this instance we're talking behaviors of avoid-ance or control. The whole purpose of the behavior is to gain short-term relief. What happens when this youngster hits a peer? The peer usually backs off, a behavior that provides relief in that moment. Or a child might run from the classroom to flee an uncomfort-

able experience. The goal is always to obtain relief *now*! When a behavior fulfills a specific need, it's programmed to continue.

4. *The child's need for relief is many times more powerful than the need to avoid consequences.* The youngster *knows* he's in big trouble after an inappropriate behavior. He can even quote the rule and the consequence chapter and verse, yet neither the rule nor the consequence prevented the behavior in the first place, nor will they prevent the behavior from happening again. More rules and more consequences simply don't work with desperate behavior. That should give us a clue.

We can try incentives and rewards for appropriate behavior, but we run into the same problem. If the child is seeking relief at a moment of internal distress, incentives and rewards for *not* acting out won't matter at all. A youngster can't be rewarded out of the behavior so long as the need for that behavior remains desperate.

5. *Some interventions actually compound the need for relief, and yet more desperate behavior.* What if some of our approaches for dealing with this child come very close to looking like the bad pictures or flash memories? If any intervention adds to the intrusive baggage the child is already toting, and if it magnifies a need for relief, it won't solve problems and issues. It can, however, make them worse.

What Needs to Happen?

Almost without exception, typical interventions for desperate behavior are tactical; they focus on behavior only, not the issues beneath it. A shift in focus involves a strategic approach (a theme you'll see again and again in this book). It's a change in focus.

In addition to addressing behavior that has already happened, we'll look at achieving that point where the youngster himself perceives and believes the inappropriate behavior is no longer necessary. Better skills will bring better behavior. (Understand I'm not inferring there should be no consequences for inappropriate behavior, only that consequences alone won't always be sufficient to prevent the behavior from happening again.)

This shift in focus, and its implementation in interventions, makes a *tremendous* difference in terms of outcomes. Isn't that what we want, better outcomes? We'll consider several areas, all skill-related, for accomplishing this change: assuring physical and emotional safety, identifying and controlling patterns in behavior, promoting skills of self-soothing, increasing tolerance for frustration, facilitating appropriate expression, and creating empowerment.

Assuring physical and emotional safety: On the surface, this one looks almost laughable. Why should we be so concerned about the safety of a youngster whose behavior threatens the welfare of everyone else?

We should be concerned because, with this youngster, perception *fuels* behavior. If a youngster feels uncomfortable or threatened, he's going to *do* something to create relief. If, for example, the child feels packed in with a bunch of other kids, or if he feels pressured to use interpersonal skills he doesn't have, a behavior that creates physical and emotional distance and isolation might well happen and continue to happen again and again. It's no surprise the behavior precisely creates the intended results. Shoving, hitting, spitting on, and yelling at peers leads to isolation. (It can lead, for instance, to exclusion from lunch recess or an imposed time-out, which creates the space the child wanted all along.)

The solution to this problem involves creating the desired relief *before* the behavior. This could involve creating more space or smaller groupings in class, especially if the youngster seems to require more distance between himself and others. Consider putting the youngster on a short task with just one other child. Give them a brief task to complete. The notion here is a success experience while working with a peer, so the task itself is of no great significance. (But keep it brief, or you'll end up with *two* kids to settle down.)

Within the classroom setting, offer the youngster a desk or seat that is not part of a row or column, but on the perimeter, the outside. This seating should be offered as an option, a choice.

Another consideration could be the creation of a "No Hassle Zone" around the youngster's desk and work space. It's a generous boundary that buffers her from the uncomfortable closeness of others. It establishes that the youngster will remain in the zone and not bother or irritate others in return for the same consideration. Again, this is presented as an option, a possible solution to the problem. (It is *not* a consequence.) As we will see in a moment, growth can happen here.

Identifying and controlling patterns in behavior: Desperate behavior tends to collect in patterns that develop and become resistant to intervention. Three characteristics, I call them the three "P"s, combine to create and strengthen these patterns:

1. *Persistent.* The behaviors don't go away.

2. *Predictable.* One can forecast the behaviors with accuracy.

3. *Pervasive.* Without intervention the behaviors spread and become even worse.

Behaviors happen, and they occur in space and time; no exceptions. There are no space-less and time-less behaviors. Anything someone *does* happens somewhere and sometime. Redirecting inappropriate behaviors and altering where and when they happen is paramount to not only stopping some of these behaviors (thus disrupting a pesky pattern), but of showing the youngster change is possible for them. These situations and interventions are covered in-depth from Chapter Sixteen to Chapter Twenty-one.

Promoting skills of self-soothing: This one is big, as the difficult child cries out for soothing. Problems develop when this youngster continually relies on others for that soothing because he cannot self-soothe well at all. (Self-soothing *is* a skill.) He doesn't know how, so he inappropriately reaches out to others for it. I call this "Taking Hostages." It's a bottomless pit, and it can grow into an enormous problem. Excessive use of drugs and alcohol, sexual addictions, and even "addiction" to games and toys represent problematic attempts to self-soothe.

Interventions for teaching self-soothing could include things like specific exercises in breath control or the use of lotions or creams as a self-applied gesture of kinesthetic soothing. These interventions and others are covered in Chapter Fifteen.

Increasing tolerance for frustration: The advantage of having daily access to a child or teen is that we can attempt to slowly build up his tolerance for frustrating events and circumstances. For example, consider the youngster who throws an assignment on the floor because he's overwhelmed with the number of problems on a page. One solution is to come in under his "radar" by limiting the problems to what he *can* manage. More problems are added gradually, or the structure of the assignment is increased in such a way that the effect of control is created. (It's also helpful to show the youngster the improvement and help him interpret it as progress.)

The student with a generous space around her, the "No Hassle Zone," probably could tolerate the space being a bit smaller on Monday morning, especially if she helps the teacher trim it down a tiny bit. It's an obvious sign of improvement, and the girl knows it.

When we help youngsters increase tolerance for frustration, we're also suggesting they can survive times of difficulty and become better at using newfound skills and insights.

Facilitating appropriate expression: The youngster with desperate behavior struggles for expression that can be questioned, interpreted, and explained. But the child or teen often is locked in images and *can't* express them. (We have a name for this condition: alexythymia. The term literally means "no words for feelings.") Frustration is compounded. Result: *More* desperate behavior occurs.

Interventions of expression include teaching the youngster a simple model and vocabulary for feelings. It begins with four feelings that can be understood by any bright two or three-year old: Sad, Mad, Glad, and Scared. The child is encouraged to interpret everyday experiences in terms of these four, with the goal of gradual improvement in the oral expression of feelings associated with daily circumstances and events. Chapter Fourteen covers these interventions.

31

Creating empowerment: The consequences of desperate behavior continually strip the youngster of power. If the child can't behave appropriately, everyday privileges and opportunities are lost (an understandable consequence). Result: There's often a sense of hopelessness and even more desperate behavior as frustration builds.

(Again, this is not intended as a criticism of consequences. It's rather a recognition that some consequences are better than others, and that even well-intended consequences don't always lead to solutions to bad behavior.)

Empowerment is created in small ways so the youngster can interpret her own progress. It might look like progress to us, but it's worth little if the child can't experience it and interpret it as personal growth.

The ability to make a choice from a menu of options would be empowering. If the youngster helps the teacher shrink the "No Hassle Zone," that's empowering. Helping someone would be empowering. Any small job or responsibility given the child can be empowering. Isn't this precisely why good kindergarten teachers always have a job for *every* student?

A teacher in Nebraska shared a story about an episode of empowerment that made a big difference for an entire school year, if not longer. She was teaching a new math concept, a tough one. Her most difficult student grasped it immediately. She smiled at him, suggesting he had a special skill for this sort of thing.

At this point the student argued with her, insisting the reason why he could do the work was because it was easy.

The teacher gently challenged him.

Easy? No; it's NOT easy. Look around you.
There are plenty of excellent students close to
you who don't understand it yet. It's NOT easy.

The boy looked around the classroom for a moment; he realized she was correct. He raised his hand.

Miss, may I help them?

Please do.

That whole exchange took less than a minute, yet the teacher reported the young man was changed from that point on in her class. His behavior and his grades climbed steadily. The boy was empowered by an observant teacher not only to be a helpful resource to others, but to understand, perhaps for the very first time, he could be a strong student, also.

Always bear in mind that one critical aspect of creating empowerment is timing; it must be accomplished when there are no behavioral issues. (Otherwise, it could look like inappropriate behavior is being rewarded. We don't want that.)

Chapter Three

Why Difficult Behavior Doesn't Change

How many times have you heard a well-intending adult say, "Well, he's just doing that for *attention*"? So?

Everyone needs and wants attention. They want to be affirmed and feel like they matter in some way. Fortunately, most folks seek their affirmation and attention in appropriate ways. Perhaps a deeper question regarding the difficult child might be, "Why do some youngsters engage in extremes of behavior in order to secure the attention and sense of significance other children obtain easily with appropriate behavior?"

That's a *good* question. Let's look into it.

Four Reasons

There are at least four characteristics that stir and maintain difficult behavior in young people: Ignorance, Fear, Thinking and Payoffs. Each of these needs to be addressed specifically if attainable and lasting change is the goal.

Ignorance: How could we possibly know what we *don't* know? How could anyone ever get a toehold on change if they have no idea of how to go about it? (Again, we're addressing missing skills.) I've met very few youngsters whom I believed schemed and planned to have their lives fall completely apart, but I've met *plenty* who improvised daily.

Emotionally intact people don't invite pain and misery; they would rather live without it. If they *knew* how to fix their lives so things would be better for them, most would have done it a long time ago. Many are ignorant; they just don't have a clue as to how to change, even when they desire it. This is especially the case with behaviorally frustrated young people.

Fear: Change involves the unknown, and the unknown can be scary. Even poor behavior brings with it a degree of predictability, a strange sort of comfort zone. Breaking out of that zone, as bad as it is, can be frightening. Add to this the fact that authentic change involves recognizing and uncovering one's vulnerabilities.

Exposing one's vulnerabilities like this can send fear off the chart. Who really *wants* to talk about their fears and insecurities? Kids certainly don't.

A huge issue with fear-based behavior is that, most often, adults address only the behavior, not the fear. Fear then hangs around, sets up residence, and orders new curtains. Nothing changes, while misery and trouble have a field day.

Thinking: Our own thoughts can beat us up plenty. Every bit of our thinking influences our behavior one way or another. We can think ourselves into isolation and depression, *expecting* negative things to happen. And, of course, they generally do.

Kids who find themselves "stuck" in inappropriate behaviors often feel they are fulfilling a role they rightly deserve. They see change as out of their reach. This thinking *must* be addressed, or behaviors won't change.

Payoffs: Poor behavior can fulfill a definite purpose even without a conscious thought or plan. If youngsters experience some sort of tangible or intangible gain from their behavior, the behavior *will* continue.

As discussed earlier, youngsters who are uncomfortable around others might, for instance, engage in behavior that keeps others at a distance. Isolation hurts, but it doesn't hurt nearly as much as the discomfort of people being painfully close.

Can you see how bad behavior might feel "good" in a sense? Can you see why it is often programmed to continue?

What Needs to Happen

Intervention for inappropriate behavior should be directed at each characteristic of Ignorance, Fear, Thinking and Payoffs.

Ignorance: Convincing a child or adolescent there are other options can be tricky business. Tell her she's ignorant, and you're likely to kick her defiance into a higher gear. No one wants that.

"Next time:" One great intervention is something Dr. William Glasser included in his original concept and applications of Reality Therapy (Glasser, 1965): "next time." (I was privileged to spend the day with Dr. Glasser back in the late seventies. It was an awesome experience in itself.)

The whole concept of "next time" infers that a behavior already acted is done; it is finished and old business. Mistakes made in the past, however, can be a springboard for better behavior when the same situation comes around again.

It's a given that an effective and well-delivered consequence should provide the message the behavior was wrong. But if the consequences stopped there, wouldn't a youngster's only desire be to avoid the next consequence? Animals can do that. Avoidance is a type of learning, but it doesn't follow much of a plan.

"Next time" focuses on the opportunity to learn from past mistakes and change them, with newfound insight, into the ability to do something different and better altogether. When combined with reasonable skill and confidence, it *will* work. It's a case of wisdom being applied to experience. It's the development of a response menu.

Intervention will be more effective, of course, if one is reasonably certain the behavior, the one that brought the consequence, is something the youngster isn't happy about, either. A failing grade on a report card would be a great example.

Most youngsters don't orchestrate well-conceived plans to fail. It simply happens. Using grades as an example, a youngster doesn't have an operational clue how to avoid failing the same class during the next reporting period. If you ask her about her plan, you might get something like this:

I'll just work HARDER on my grades!

What kind of a plan is that? I've worked with plenty of kids who made such a vague statement their whole approach to improvement. They made it work for a couple of weeks, then the same old problems paid a visit.

A plan-making strategy: Make an appointment to discuss options of a plan with the youngster. It helps to let her work a time out with you that's at least a couple of days away. That way, there's less apprehension and questions about the appointment when it is made. It also gives her some time to think about school and her grades. She can select from some suggested times or, if she offers a suggestion that works for you, go with it. It also helps to set a time limit on the "appointment" up front, so she won't see it as going on forever. (The whole idea is for her to see value in these quick meetings rather than dread them.) Remember, the more she's involved in the process, the more interested and empowered she'll be in arriving at a solution.

At the meeting, ask her what she plans to do that would create better outcomes for her at the end of the next reporting period. Encourage her to come up with three very specific alternatives that would lead to a better outcome "next time."

Young people often get stuck on this. They might think of one and perhaps crank out a second, but three are tough.

It's best (for them and for the sake of avoiding an argument) if she can come up with three on her own. If you were to *tell* her three things she could do to pass all the classes next time, you would be giving her *your* plan, not hers. There would be little interest or desire to follow it.

If she does get stuck, or can't be specific enough, there are two options:

> 1. *Encourage her to keep thinking about it, then set up another appointment to meet again on the matter.* Sometimes the thought of another "appointment" brings a second or third response quickly!

> 2. *Ask if she'd like a suggestion or two.* Asking serves two purposes. First, it solicits her permission, an empowering gesture that should not go unnoticed. Second, if she wants to argue or disagree with any of your suggestions, simply back out of the conflict by saying, "Well, you said you wanted some suggestions."

In helping her come up with a plan for implementing alternatives for change (examples might include getting up earlier in the morning, holding to a specific time and place to study, or developing a better system for tracking assignments), include a timetable for their achievement, plus clear ways for evaluating their effectiveness. Set a time to meet again to check on progress and make changes, where needed.

Fear: Any sort of change involves stepping into the unknown. Few things are scarier than the unknown. Living well involves living with vulnerability and exposing our most tender emotional parts from time to time.

Since the best components of our lives involve relationships, and since relationships always involve vulnerability, any effort to reduce risk and vulnerability easily can diminish relationships. For that reason, fear keeps a lot of folks stuck, afraid to move in *any* direction. In the meantime, their relationships suffer.

Fearful people can be terrified of change. They're afraid to change, yet they're petrified about *not* changing. Again, they're stuck.

The new arrival: I saw an example of this sort of fear once while a psychologist in a drug and alcohol treatment program. A new patient arrived, a muscled, healthy-looking, construction worker in his mid-20s. He had traveled from New Jersey to Dilley, Texas, to either deal with cocaine or to die. (Folks who don't realize those two options battle for the same parking space know little about addiction.)

When he checked into his room there at the hospital, he noticed there were no sheets on his bed. Immediately, he barged into his counselor's office and demanded the sheets.

The counselor, a burly, no-nonsense guy with 20+ years of sobriety, came around his desk. He removed his cigarette and walked straight into the young man's face.

Are you talking to ME?

The patient broke down and wept like a baby. He was terrified. (Where it mattered most, *all* the patients were terrified.)

Normalizing fear: I could go on and on about fear, but let's direct our attention at dealing with it with young people. It can be a challenge because, from their perspective, it's *not* good to be afraid, even appropriately so. Younger children tend to be more realistic about things that frighten them, while peer pressure with adolescents sends a message that fear is something awful.

It's not, of course, and I would start there. I would "normalize" fear for the youngster:

> *You know, fear has been described as The Guide to Wisdom. That means it's good and normal to be afraid sometimes, especially when we feel physically or emotionally threatened. It's fear that keeps us from playing with rattlesnakes, drinking poison, or trying to jump the Grand Canyon in a tricycle. It's not a very fun emotion, but a very necessary and appropriate one. What kind of things would frighten you?*

Some youngsters might balk at this question because, in a way, they've been set up. To say they are not afraid of anything would be to infer they are *not* normal or appropriate. From there, it's generally not too difficult to discuss different things, past and present, that make them fearful and uncomfortable. As rapport deepens, so does their authentic recognition of fear and, hopefully, what they can do about it.

It takes courage to make that first move against fear. Courage should always be recognized and validated.

Bear in mind that you sometimes will have the opposite problem: the youngster who is afraid of *everything*. With that child, I would go through the fears and help them identify ways they can address them and cut the fears down to size. Again, courage is a player.

Thinking: Of the four reasons why difficult behavior doesn't change, the most challenging one is thinking. What and how a person thinks is deeply personal and can be resistant to intervention. Thinking doesn't even have to fit with the reality of the situation for it to make perfect sense to a youngster. Thinking, therefore, fuels behavior.

A rush to Rushmore: By way of an example, my work once took me to Rapid City, South Dakota, so I naturally made the short, sight-seeing trip to Keystone. I arrived at Mount Rushmore early one evening, only to find the whole place engulfed in fog.

The huge spotlights were pointed straight at the presidents there in the granite, but their light could not penetrate the dense fog. I was disappointed. I promised myself I'd see them on my next trip to the area, and I did.

But what if I had taken the arrogant stance that said, "If I can't see them, they're *not* there." Such a stance would not have changed the reality of the place one bit, but it would have changed my thinking and my behavior about Mount Rushmore. Why on earth should I go back if the presidents aren't there?

It's much the same with a youngster whose behavior is based on misperception and faulty thinking. A little fog and fuzziness in the world can alter many things.

Does this mean youngsters will engage in inappropriate behavior over and over again, even when there is no rationale for it? Of course; it happens all the time.

Four reasons: There are at least four reasons why thinking can be a component of difficult behavior:

1. *Pressure to NOT think.* Children from pathologically compulsive families learn quickly that thinking is dangerous. The way to survive means to be compliant ... or else. In the dysfunctional home, children *must* follow these directives: *Don't ever THINK, Don't ever FEEL, Don't ever TELL,* and *Don't ever LOSE CONTROL.* So they suffer in silence. To challenge any of these mandates is to risk catastrophe. (One possible exception is the really young child, who will tell you just about anything. They quickly learn, however, what *not* to talk about.)

2. *Rigidity.* This describes the youngster who truly thinks everything *must* fall into compartments of black or white; nothing else. If a child feels everyone in the world is demanding something from him, he probably won't give it. He'll blame continued poor behavior on the intent of others toward him. As a result, he'll create the outcomes he already expects. This youngster will use actions of adults that fit his thinking as evidence that he is correct. The compartmentalization of people and circumstances, whether they fit in the boxes prepared for them or not, is a serious hindrance to change.

3. *Risk.* To change one's thinking about the role, actions, and intent of others is to change one's behavior accordingly. The tendency is toward no change at all. After all, change means being vulnerable and the possibility of being wrong. Both of these are uncomfort-

able; *not* taking a risk is safer. (I do believe, however, that youngsters sometimes beat themselves up for not exercising the courage to change. Adults are no different.)

4. *Blatant arrogance.* Dr. Doug Riley discusses this one in his best-seller, *The Defiant Child* (Riley, 1997). He suggests some youngsters consider themselves the equal to the adults in their lives. They *know* how to fight the wars and win the battles. Why would they want to stop?

So what is the solution for changing a youngster's thinking? In short, we should make it as easy as possible for a youngster to change thinking and behavior, and proceed from there.

Changing the mindset: Encouragement for a youngster to change starts by *not* talking about it; most kids think we're all talk, anyway. Here's a case for actions speaking more powerfully than words. Affirm the child in small ways that have no "catch" or expectation attached to them at all, as they are expecting a "But ..." to drop in there somewhere.

Even if you must ask the youngster to do a chore or task, such as bringing the empty garbage cans around to the back, make it a separate request later. If the youngster is cutting the grass or raking leaves, for instance, take them a glass of ice water or an ice cream sandwich with a smile. Don't say anything! Keep it up and, over time, thinking *will* be affected.

The same thing holds true in the school environment. Sally might see her teacher waiting for her at her locker. Sally is expecting some sort of "lecture" about what she has done, or hasn't done (probably for good reason). Actually, the teacher was waiting to congratulate Sally on her new baby brother. Result: Sally was *wrong* about her teacher's intent. What's more, Sally *knows* she was wrong. Don't you think this shift in thinking eventually might show up in Sally's behavior?

(Bear in mind some adults might consider these gestures to be a waste of time in light of their need for *immediate* change. To me, it amounts to the difference in solving a problem once, then having to address it repeatedly, or making enough of an impact in a youngster's perception that a problem is solved *permanently* over time. This is precisely why not every adult is struggling with this youngster. Permanent changes in behavior can *only* follow permanent changes in thinking.)

This is how a mindset regarding adults and resistant behavior toward them is changed. It happens a little at a time.

Consider, also, how we might gain compliance from a youngster, and yet *never* change how they think. What would that mean? It would make every compliant behavior an isolated event. The youngster would never perceive fully the benefits or rationale of self-directed change. It amounts to putting out maximum effort for minimal compliance, and doing it over and over and over again. That's a *lot* of work, especially if there's a better way.

Is it possible a youngster might make a rigid-thought statement like, "Everybody hates me!" in order to entangle a parent, teacher, or counselor into an argument they can win? What do you think?

If you're pretty sure the youngster doesn't really believe what he is saying, it's probably not worth being drawn into a discussion about it. Consider letting it go; save your energy for a bigger crisis.

Constructing an exception: On the other hand, the youngster might really *believe* everyone hates him! Consider challenging him with a dialog that constructs a single exception to his thinking, an exception he can't dismantle.

Tommy, you say that EVERYONE hates you?

Uh,huh ... everybody!

Nobody likes you?

Nobody.

I see, Tommy, I understand you went to your grandmother's for spring break.

I did.

Did you enjoy going to her place? I understand she lives on a farm.

I liked it so much I didn't want to leave.

I understand, Tommy. But you know what? It makes me kind of sad to think you spent the whole week with someone who HATES you.

WHAT??? My grandmother doesn't HATE me!

*She must, Tommy, because you just told me
EVERYBODY hates you. Your grandmother
is part of everybody, right?*

No ... not really.

*Do you mean that everybody hates you
EXCEPT your grandmother?*

Yeah, everybody ... but NOT my grandmother.

*Well, that's good, Tommy. Knowing your
grandmother doesn't hate you helps a little,
doesn't it?*

Yeah, I guess.

In this brief exchange Tommy had to come up with another
box labeled, "People who DON'T hate me." At first, Grandma is
in there all by herself. Over time, Tommy could be encouraged to
give Grandma some company: other folks who don't hate him.
The aim would be for Tommy to come to the conclusion that it's
not *everybody* who hates him.

Of course, it might be prudent to help Tommy with his social
skills, also.

Payoffs: Who knows why any inappropriate behavior happens for the first time? There could be multiple reasons, or it
could be an isolated event, just one of those things. If it happens

again, however, and then again and again, it's a safe bet there's a payoff for that behavior hiding somewhere just below the surface. After all, what would be the purpose of repeating a behavior that accomplishes nothing?

(Note: We're barely scratching the surface here. In Chapter Twenty we will dig deeply into payoffs and outcomes. We will look at how they can drive inappropriate behavior.)

Payoffs can keep poor behavior going on forever. They must be addressed or little change will be realized. There are two kinds of payoffs: tangible and intangible.

Tangible: Whenever a young child tells a lie for the first time and it works, the kid feels like he has invented a marvelous way to get an ice cream bar when he really *didn't* pick up his room or feed the dog. This lie business works pretty well until he discovers that telling a fib can carry a steep price. (As a kid growing up in the Bible Belt, I didn't know much about murder, assault, or armed robbery. My grandmother had me convinced that lying was the *worst* possible thing a person could do. I still have strong personal feelings about it. I can handle a lot of things, but I cannot tolerate a liar.) Too many individuals had to learn the hard way that lying can buy you some neat stuff today, but a ton of trouble tomorrow.

What about kids who extort stuff from their parents or their siblings and peers? I worked with a young man who didn't like the back-to-school shoes his mother had picked out for him. He wanted baseball cleats. (To be accurate, the cleats are the special grippers on the soles of athletic shoes, but folks generally call the shoes themselves "cleats.") As Mom held firm, the boy went into a tirade on the spot. He threatened to trash the whole shoe store if he didn't get the cleats.

Well, he got his baseball shoes but, more importantly, he learned he could get a lot of neat stuff if he could run a good bluff and threaten enough people. Sometimes, however, it was *not* a bluff. (We'll revisit this young man later.)

Our children don't have to be dismantling a shoe store to come up with less-than-appropriate ways of getting what they want. They can be quite creative. Strategies that work the best on parents and teachers are filed away for repeat performances.

The solution is neither easy nor comfortable, but it *will* work: Hold tough, no matter what. Behavior that doesn't achieve a pay-off will eventually (and hopefully) fall away.

Intangible: Sometimes a youngster's behavior is intended to draw a response from others that is self-serving to the youngster. There are two kinds of intangible behaviors: controlling behaviors and distancing behaviors.

Controlling behaviors range from criticism and put-downs to outright bullying. These mean-spirited behaviors are designed to gain at the expense of everyone else. These kids feed on the pain of others.

Consider, also, the payoff a youngster receives from irritating and annoying others, especially authority figures. When this kid sees the exasperation in an adult's face, it's like he's being paid off in gold.

Distancing behaviors can be extremely resistant to change precisely because they *are* so effective. There are some youngsters who don't want anyone getting close to them. Their emotional and physical boundaries are not to be breached; period. When another youngster gets too close for comfort, this child is apt to push them away with a caustic word or action ("Get away from me"! "Leave me alone"! or a hard shove that delivers the message.)

What happens then? The other youngster backs off, right? That's a payoff; the behavior fulfilled its intent perfectly.

It *will* happen again.

(The "gain" of distance and space from others is a valid reinforcer of behavior. In Chapter Twenty, however, we'll see where this same behavior also amounts to the avoidance of closeness in relationships.)

Managing payoffs: In terms of intervention, the obvious solution is to eliminate the payoffs. But this is much easier said than done. We don't always have full control over every situation and circumstance. I've seen and heard of parents holding firm on a tantrum-bent child, only to draw unfavorable attention from mall security. It can be a tough call, and some youngsters are talented enough to draw a payoff from most *any* situation. (It's what they do, and they're *good* at it.)

If a doctor or therapist instructs parents to use interventions like therapeutic holding with an out-of-control child, it would be advised the parent carry a letter from the therapist explaining the intervention and the need for it. The letter could help if parents are questioned by the authorities.

If a child tends to stretch the truth about things like completed chores or homework, she should be expected to offer proof of her compliance before the bargain is completed.

Completion of school work doesn't always mean it gets turned in. You might want to check that out, also. (My son worked and went to college part-time. I offered to pay his tuition, but only after seeing his grades from the previous semester. I believe it worked out well for both of us: He had some help with school, and I had reasonable assurance I wasn't throwing my money away.)

Reducing arguments: Keep in mind that a youngster who wants to argue will do it as long as it works. As often as not, arguments escalate until the insults and the defiance become the bigger issue. A response like, "I know you don't like it, but that's my decision," coupled with a hasty exit, is the preferred strategy. And, since some kids will follow Mom or Dad from room to room with an argument, an exit that takes the parent out the driveway isn't a bad option. Hint: *Always* have an "exit" plan in mind, if possible.

If you believe a youngster is into distancing behavior, you might experiment with ways to approach the child without him becoming upset. Respect boundaries when you can. They are real, and they differ from person to person. It might be helpful to discuss boundaries with the youngster, and work out a solution both of you can honor.

A poker face works pretty well with the youngster who is watching you for signs of frustration. Practice; it can pare down the payoff and move you a bit closer to a solution.

Chapter Four

The Victim Game

Difficult and defiant behavior guarantees a victim is close. In fact, continued conflict *requires* a victim. Think about that. If there isn't at least one victim, there can't be a conflict.

Attack of the Victims

It would be difficult, impossible really, to discuss the inappropriate behavior of a child or teen without considering the self-destroying aspect of becoming a victim. Every person who acts out against another person considers themselves a victim of some sort. They feel put upon, hurt (physically or emotionally), and embarrassed. They also feel as if they're being put into a position of "less than," a condition of scarcity. It all contributes to why youngsters act out.

The high cost of winning: Winning became a biological imperative when man first stepped out of his cave only to meet up with a sabre-tooth tiger. Losing back then didn't mean you went home without tiger steaks for dinner; it meant you *became* the dinner. The need to win was paramount; the stakes were pretty high, and losing had a dear cost. Unfortunately, a lot of humans still carry a lot of that cave person around with them every day. To the youngster caught up in this need, winning and surviving mean the *same* thing.

(My reference to victims here is directed toward those individuals who claim victimhood as their lifestyle instead of dealing with their problems head-on. I'm *not* referring to legitimate victims, such as youngsters who are abused or neglected.)

Blame warfare: If victims are perceived as losers, what happens when two victims go at it, each one bound and determined to win regardless of the cost? I believe it will result in the desperate behavior I mentioned earlier. The outcome would be a youngster who behaves aggressively and inappropriately, clearly looking like an abuser, but *feeling* very much like a victim.

Are we saying that a youngster can play both roles, abuser and victim, at the *same* time? Absolutely.

Victims have little or no power because they must blame their problems on someone or something else. Since their shortcomings are never their fault, they fail to see how they could be empowered to change their circumstances. They're trapped.

It's much easier and less risky to be a victim than to do something about it. It's not a fun place to be, but it's safe (in a sense), and it's incredibly consistent. Nothing is ever that person's fault; it's up to everyone *else* to change. How likely is that to happen?

The simple downside to this sort of thinking is that it doesn't work over time. I've actually encountered folks, adults as well as kids, who didn't *want* to be empowered to solve their problems because, if their efforts didn't work, they would be fresh out of others to blame for their failure. For them to step out of blame would be to step into responsibility.

And how scary would that be?

Scarcity

Victims make a steady diet of scarcity. It's a way of life; they *need* it to justify their misery. If they don't have enough money, it's not because they lack industry, drive, or hustle; it's because everything is too expensive. If they don't have any friends, it isn't because they haven't worked at making themselves more friendly and approachable; it's because everyone is so mean and hateful to them all the time. If they have trouble with academics, it's not because they don't study, ask for help, and put extra effort into their studies; it's because school is simply too hard or the teacher just doesn't like them.

Have you ever heard any of these blame-based excuses coming from a young person? The problem with scarcity is there's *plenty* of it.

Fixing It Takes WORK

Empowerment defeats the victim mentality and the scarcity merry-go-round. Empowerment means having a plan, and it means some work. One must break a sweat to make it happen.

A foot on the table: A few years back I attended a speakers' convention in San Diego. The event involved a nice, sit-down dinner. As everyone at the table engaged in conversation about the day's events, one of the table guests put his bare foot right smack down on the table.

"Disgusting," most folks would think. "What a way to ruin a nice dinner."

But what if that dinner guest had no arms? That changes things, doesn't it? In truth, this man ate, drank, took notes, and even wrote a book with his feet. His attitude through it all was positive and pleasantly infectious. Both his accomplishments and his attitude came with deliberate planning and effort.

Did this man experience scarcity? Well, not having your arms would qualify as a scarcity, I believe. But he was far from being powerless, and light years from being a victim. As a matter of fact, he is a powerful speaker on the topic of dealing with adversity. He is an inspiration wherever he goes. He certainly inspired me. I challenge you to find a better example of someone who walks his talk, and enjoys the benefits of doing so.

The difference, the total difference, really, amounts to what happens between one's ears. *Every* behavior, good or bad, starts right there.

What Needs to Happen?

It's a fact that adults play the victim and wallow in their scarcity much more than kids, but they do it in *front* of their children. Young people are affected by example, an example they too often follow themselves. For this reason, children and teens need to be exposed to empowering, victim-busting, responsibility-based examples and activities.

Empowerment, responsibility, and risk: As an individual feels less a victim and more in control, he will be less fearful, less angry, and more appropriate in essentially every way. That's a given; it's safe to offer as a guarantee. The whole notion of scarcity, victim status, and victim thinking fades quickly when replaced with empowerment. Empowerment serves as the key that frees feelings and actions of helplessness.

Empowerment involves responsibility and risk. Both are trouble for scarcity-driven young people. It feels better to remain a victim than to act and risk failure. This is precisely why a lot of kids stay "stuck" in the victim mode. It's miserable, but it's safe.

Should we attempt to remove the responsibility and risk youngsters face in achieving more control and empowerment in their lives? I don't think so. We can, however, help them realize as much as possible from the efforts they do make.

The magic of asking: Let's say there's a shop down the street that sells vacuum cleaners and supplies. It's owned by an elderly couple who've owned the shop for many years. One day, as you're buying a few bags for your machine at home, the old gentleman mentions how he's not up to cleaning the dirt, snow, and leaves off his sidewalk and driveway anymore.

He knows you work with young people and asks if you know of a young man or young lady who might like the job. It pays well, and it only takes a couple of hours twice a week after school. He makes it clear that, if you know of a good candidate for the position, the job is theirs.

You know just the person. He's been complaining about how he'd like to earn a little extra money, but up to now, that's about all he's been doing: complaining. You tell him about the couple with the shop and how they're looking for some help. You suggest he pay them a visit, adding he could mention your name.

This job is as close to automatic as it could possibly be. All he has to do is show up and *ask*! That would get him the job. But he has to do two critically important (and risky *and* scary) things: 1) show up, and 2) ask.

Here's a situation where, unknown to the youngster, you have ensured an outcome, but he does have to show *some* initiative and effort. Hopefully, a good outcome will encourage even more initiative and effort as the youngster gains in skill and confidence. In the process, he should be less fearful and apprehensive about future risks and gestures of this sort.

You can't have it BOTH ways (Ruben's Paradox): Here's a strategy to use with a child or teen who is especially slippery when it comes to taking responsibility. I call it Ruben's Paradox.

Ruben (not his real name) got into so much trouble at school the principal offered him this deal:

If you get into even one more fight at school, I will suspend you for three days. Do you understand?

Ruben indicated he did understand; he was able to repeat the "deal" back to the principal.

The very next morning, Ruben got into another fight before school even started. The principal was *not* happy.

What am I going to do about this, Ruben?

Suspend me for three days?

Did you think I was joking?

No, Sir?

What were you thinking when you came to school this morning?

That I should have a good day, and not get into any more trouble?

That was a pretty good plan, Ruben. What happened?

Jimmy made me mad, so I hit him.

So Jimmy made you get into trouble?

Yes, sir, he did.

Ruben, can other people MAKE you do things you don't want to do?

No, sir. Nobody can MAKE me do nothing I don't want to do.

Well, Ruben, you DID get into trouble for fighting the morning after we talked about it. That means one of two things happened: Either you were never serious about staying out of trouble this morning OR, indeed, people can sometimes MAKE you do things you don't want to do. It's one or the other, Ruben. Which one is it?

Although Ruben has a choice here (and it is critical that he voice one), either choice takes him in a direction he *doesn't* want to go, a direction of looking at his own thoughts and actions. And it leaves him with some work to do.

An empowering apology: Another example might involve an apology, something else that's difficult for this youngster. Let's say a girl acts out inappropriately in class or walks through a neighbor's flower bed. Although she did wrong, and knows it, Susan's afraid that, if she approaches the teacher or the neighbor with an apology, they'd be very upset with her.

Here's where telling the teacher or the neighbor Susan will be speaking with them about her behavior could soften the situation for the girl. A good outcome could help a lot, but Susan still has to show up and make the effort.

A good "I": Another strategy for minimizing blame and reducing the victim thing comes from the late Thomas Gordon, the founder and author of PET, *Parent Effectiveness Training* (Gordon, 1970). It's a decades-old approach called the "I" Message.

During issues of conflict or disagreement with others, a person is encouraged to use "I" in addressing the problem rather than "You." "You" is more coercive and blaming:

> *YOU forgot all about coming over and helping me study for the algebra test last night! YOU didn't want to do it, anyway.*

"I" can accomplish the same thing, but without "attacking" the other person:

> *I became worried when you didn't come over last night and help me study for the algebra test. I was concerned that you might have been in an accident.*

In this example the person admits to being worried and concerned, leaving it up to the other person to explain their absence. In a sensitive way, it puts the responsibility where it needs to be, but without the accusation.

When I explain this approach to young people, I tell them that, regardless of the issue or conflict, there's *always* a way to package it into an "I" Message:

It really scared me when ...

I was embarrassed when ...

I laughed so hard I cried when ...

It worried me a lot when ...

I became pretty upset when ...

I was so disappointed when ...

Remember, "I" represents a type of responsibility, also. It reflects a responsibility for one's thoughts and conclusions. That's a good thing.

Challenging fear and insecurity: What we're really addressing here is the ability to live "straight up" and squarely face those issues that hang dangerously close to fear and insecurity. As responsible adults, we should demonstrate to our children how we call the mortgage company *before* we can't make the house payment, or how we work a problem out with the boss *before* he shows up in our doorway. These actions take some courage, and courage comes with practice. Suggestion: Give them *lots* of practice.

Management of conflict: We could also help youngsters understand that the effectiveness of handling a disagreement or conflict with another person is a skill that can be learned and practiced. It's a direct approach for reducing trouble; it can lead to one being recognized as having exceptional interpersonal skills. Chapter Twenty-two, *Mastering Noncoercive Response*, has some great ideas for improving and polishing these skills.

Chapter Five

Anger: Racing Fuel for Conflict

Anger is a valid emotion, a key component to achieving emotional equilibrium. Without anger, we would tend to be passive in situations that call for action. Anger is necessary for healthy self-esteem and all aspects of respect for self and relationships with others.

Stuck in the "On" Position

But anger was never intended to be stuck in the "On" position. (Imagine a light switch you could never turn off.) Too much of it for too long is harmful. It can rob a person of the opportunity to resolve issues that caused the anger to surface in the first place. Anger is one of those short-term emotions that, unfortunately, can grow into a long-term (inappropriate) tool for managing relationships.

In every case I can think of, long-term, stuck-in-the-"On" position anger targets people rather than things. If our car doesn't start on a cold winter morning, we might be upset at the car. But we'd consider a person rather strange if 20 years later they were *still* angry at the car for that one morning's nonperformance. But it's not at all uncommon for folks to be angry at certain individuals for 20, 30, even 40 years, or more.

Chronic anger is also unhealthy. When prolonged anger creates sleep difficulties for a youngster, alertness and vitality at school are compromised. Results: Poor grades and other achievement difficulties are noted. Over the years, unresolved anger contributes to an overall decline in health (hypertension, ulcers and disease).

Four Reasons Why Anger Hangs Around

Any behavior, good or bad, continues because of a perceived value or advantage. From a youngster's perspective, staying angry might work better (at least in the short-term) than putting it aside.

It's the component of relationships that causes anger to become stuck. There are at least four reasons why a youngster might choose to remain angry rather than resolve it: Distance, Control, Release, and Insulation. All the instruction, education, and lecturing in the world isn't going to phase a child or adolescent whose anger is being strengthened and reinforced.

Distance: Anger keeps folks from getting too close. Closeness in relationships with peers and key adults *always* requires a degree of vulnerability. The angry child feels too vulnerable already. As long as she can keep others at bay with her behavior, she doesn't have to worry as much about others not liking her, and she certainly doesn't have to worry about anyone approaching her.

"They don't like me because I hit them (or yell at them, or spit on them)," she might say to herself. Although it's a lousy way to manage people, it does soften thoughts of being unlikable. And, if you think about it, anger can be a passable disguise for poor social skills. Keeping folks away then becomes a chronic practice. It's miserable, but it's effective.

Sometimes these "anger barriers" are more subtle: facial expressions and body language that keep others away, or even the way a child chooses to physically separate herself from others in a group setting. This youngster is in what I call a "psycho-behavioral bind." They want to be liked, but they can't risk rejection. They're stuck.

Control: Angry behavior can dominate circumstances completely. The child who acts out might be doing so to alter immediate events, to change outcomes. It's a deliberate fire in the trash basket. It won't do much damage, but it redirects everyone's attention. A boy can't read, so he acts out when asked to read aloud in class. The rationale here is an example of simple survival: It's better to be labeled a troublemaker than pegged as a kid who can't read. (We'll look at this behavior again later.) This same dynamic applies to a number of skills and competencies.

Release: In a very authentic sense, angry behavior feels *good*. Frustration is released and adrenaline gets a workout. It's possible for a youngster (and *definitely* for an adult) to chase the "rush" they experience with their own angry behavior. (In the case of adults, issues with rageful behavior can become every bit as serious as addiction to drugs and alcohol.)

Insulation: Anger blankets vulnerability and protects our fears and insecurities from further damage and hurt. In fact, it's a safe bet that youngsters who act out regularly are insecure and afraid. Their anger keeps the lid on the box that contains the stuff that still hurts plenty. They don't want to look at the tender vulnerabilities that are inside. (For that matter, who does?) For them, repeated consequences for their misbehavior are less painful than looking into that box. If we are not careful, our response to the child's anger only will serve to put another nail or two through the lid that keeps that box closed tight.

What Needs to Happen?

First of all, most folks don't *want* to live in a constant state of anger and turmoil. It makes people sick. Unfortunately, these four provide powerful payoffs for angry behavior, even to the point where chronic anger begins to feel "comfortable."

What person in their right mind would want to be on a three-day road trip with someone like this?

Distance: Granted, some folks (and I'm one of them) just want a little space when they are upset. Problems can erupt when that demand for space becomes never-ending and inappropriate. It can even become abusive.

An upset youngster who says, "Get out of my face; leave me alone!" is likely referring to the moment, not a long-term withdrawal from the relationship. (In fact, some of these kids later regret the way they treated their friends in their moment of misery. That's a good thing, as that child doesn't need to be convinced he was wrong.)

Can a child gain a bit of space during a stressful time and not be hurtful in the process? Of course. Here's a sample, teachable dialog. It starts with a youngster putting a hand up as a friend approaches:

> *I really don't want to talk about it right now, okay? Maybe later; I just need a little space right now.*

A dialog like this accomplishes the distance while offering a bit of credit to the good intent of the friend. Additionally, I would encourage the youngster to approach the friend later (when she's no longer upset) to let the friend know *they* were not the problem.

This can be role-played easily enough. It builds upon the message that being upset does not give one license to hurt others.

Consider, also, that some kids have larger than usual personal boundaries, especially when they are upset. Attention devoted to helping a youngster identify and better manage these boundaries can be quite productive.

Control: In this context we're addressing the need youngsters have to control an immediate outcome. In fact, they often feel they *must* control it or experience something extremely uncomfortable. We have all felt that way from time to time, but this kid *lives* in a fairly constant state of discomfort about something.

Anger and aggression can redirect the insecurities of the moment, but they create a whole new pack of problems. Anger can, of course, bubble up from deep-seated issues, but long-term anger usually connects with an inability to resolve it. It's a deficiency in cognitive, social, or emotional skills.

It's possible to encourage youngsters to "borrow" or exchange skills. Let's say, for instance, that our angry youngster is good at drawing, and the child we pair him with is good at reading and explaining things to the class. The two work on a project that results in a hand-drawn poster and a presentation to the class about sharks, or whatever. Both are involved, and both get to showcase their strongest skills.

Therapists will tell you youngsters don't enjoy focusing on their shortcomings. This is precisely why visits to a counselor might not make it past the first session. Children and teens can become excited, however, about learning and using newfound skills. Result: New skills and competencies reduce the need to overcontrol everything and everyone, and there's less anger.

When I was doing a *lot* of therapy with kids, I would often close a session by teaching them a simple but impressive magic trick (a new skill). The results were immediate and powerful. They could now do something their friends *couldn't* do. It was a shot of skills tonic. (Then, before they left, I'd show them a neat trick I would teach them in the *next* session. That usually brought them back.)

Another approach in dealing with a control-type of anger or disruption is to show the youngster that the issue will not disappear or go away because of their behavior. At some point it will have to be addressed.

Bottom line: Assess and address skills. Start big or start small; just start.

Release: Anger as a release is like popping a balloon. As much fun as it might be, it destroys the balloon. That instant of, "I like how this feels!" is definitely a high. Believe me, there are folks who will chase that high *regardless* of the trouble that follows it. This makes anger as a release the most difficult of the four to manage.

Intervention should come in two parts. The first is consequence-driven change; the second addresses the benefits of living with less anger and aggression.

Consequence-driven change: This is the realization that an instant of release might not be worth the grief it brings. Every kid understands this *after* they've gotten into trouble, again. The real accomplishment is to get them to the point where they realize it *before* they explode.

Benefits of less anger: This part of the intervention points to the realization that, with better insight and improved skills, *not* being angry has strong benefits. When I worked with adults in 28-day, inpatient treatment for drug and alcohol addiction, we gave patients a break halfway through treatment. We took them on a day of sight-seeing and great Mexican food in San Antonio.

Every single patient came to an awesome therapeutic conclusion: They could have a *lot* of fun and enjoyment in life *without* drugs and alcohol. It was a turning point in their treatment. It works with children and teens, also. Life without chronic anger *is* the way to go.

Consider asking the youngster a question like this: "What would it mean to wake up in the morning and *not* be angry at all, and *know* you could go all day with no trouble at all?" My guess is no one has ever asked that question. So ask; then follow up.

Insulation: If "release" is the toughest of the four for intervention, "insulation" is the easiest and most direct. After all, there's more than enough hurt, pain, ridicule, and embarrassment in this world to go around. They are *not* unique experiences, although youngsters often feel they are. A layer of insulation placed over the hurt ("I don't care!") might take away some of the sting, but the youngster generally knows what the sting is.

Intervention isn't rocket science. It doesn't need to be. In fact, empathetic folks who haven't had a day of training in it can help friends dig out of their hurt. What's more, they can do it very well.

How do I find out what's under the insulation, the "I don't care!" when the youngster really *does* care? I ask. I have found that, if the angry child is already upset or tearful, those very emotions make an excellent entry point for talking about feelings, especially since the feelings are right there in your lap.

When a youngster senses you care, that you want to help them, and that you *can* help them, they are usually cooperative in ways that might surprise you.

Chapter Six

The Behavior Modification Trap

Parents and teachers have used tangible rewards and incentives with children and teens for years. The time eventually comes, however, when these reinforcers backfire with difficult and defiant youngsters. At first glance, the reasons for the ineffectiveness of tangible rewards and incentives seem puzzling and unclear. The frustration on the faces of the adults, however, couldn't be clearer.

I once received an email from a concerned mother of an ODD child. Instead of asking for ideas for managing her son's defiance and noncompliance, she specifically requested the best behavior modification approaches (the systematic use of rewards and incentives) to use with the boy.

She was surprised, I'm sure, at my reply. I suggested to her that I might not recommend any behavior modification interventions at all. (To read my entire response to this mother's email, check out the article, "Treatment for ODD: Behavior Modification, or Something Else?" in the free articles section of my website at www.docspeak.com.)

Is it Oversold?

It probably *is* oversold. When I was taking all those Special Education classes for teachers in college, the rave of the age was behavior modification. It grew from the work and research of Dr. B.F. Skinner. The message of behavior modification stated you could direct behavior and instill learning through the manipulation of reinforcement (rewards) given in appropriate "schedules" (amounts and intervals). The "secret" in making behavior modification work effectively was the establishment of clear baselines (the nature of the behavior as intervention starts) and systematic reinforcement schedules, a process referred to as contingency management.

(Done appropriately, behavior modification is a *lot* of work. I know; I had to do a project in one of those classes. I used pieces of cheese to teach my dog to come immediately whenever I blew a whistle. I charted it and everything. It worked! McKeeford eventually came running on the first tweet of the whistle. In fact, it worked so well that, for weeks after the project was over, *any* whistle had him looking for cheese!)

Limitations

At one point behavior modification was billed as the panacea, the magical solution for changing behavior. After all, if you've ever seen a chicken play basketball or watched the amazing stuff Shamu can do, it's pretty impressive. As an intervention with oppositional and defiant youngsters, however, behavior modification has its limitations, although there are folks around who think differently. In my opinion, the limitations are not in the process of how authentic behavior modification employing rewards and incentives are used, rather in the purpose and application of the person implementing the intervention.

Read just about anything I've written over the last 30 years or so and you won't see much on charts, stars, and rewards for improving behavior or responsibility. It's not because those things are inherently bad or wrong. It's that, for some youngsters, an approach based primarily on earning rewards for compliance is too incomplete to foster lasting change and promote a mindset for keeping the change going and lasting. Add to this the problem of dealing with Johnny when he *doesn't* get his star, widget, or whatever, and pitches a walleyed fit about it.

Issues to Consider

Behavior modification has its place in supporting and sustaining changed behavior, but doesn't have *all* the answers. In some cases, it might have characteristics that actually *feed* into a youngster's willful defiance. Here are some things to think about when considering tangible rewards and incentives as an intervention for difficult and defiant behavior.

Depth of intervention: Behavior modification manages surface behaviors pretty well, but it doesn't go very deep. It can encourage desired behaviors to be repeated, but behavior modification doesn't take into account what might be fueling the defiance in the first place.

Oppositional Defiant Disorder as a condition rarely occurs in isolation. Research has shown that as many as half of the youngsters diagnosed as ODD also could be significantly depressed (Wenning et al., 1993). In fact, an additional diagnosis of depression could be given in many instances. (We'll stay with depression for the sake of this point, but a number of conditions and diagnoses can coexist with ODD.)

So what does this mean, exactly? It means, although behavior modification could improve some of the behaviors of a depressed and defiant youngster, there's a risk of missing a better opportunity for intervention. It's also possible the child or teen could think we care *only* that they behave and comply, that we are oblivious to how awful and miserable they feel. Result: The behaviors worsen.

If a child is defiant *and* depressed, we should work on the depression first. The defiance might go away. This is precisely why a comprehensive psychological assessment, complete with projective testing, is so helpful.

Unseen payoffs: What about the power of "invisible" payoffs that counter your efforts? What if we fail to see what *other* reinforcers are already on the plate? If we tell Johnny that he can have an ice cream cone at the end of the day if he doesn't bloody Mark's nose again like yesterday, how do we deal with the fact that bloodying Mark's nose was exactly what *made* Johnny's day yesterday?

And he's supposed to trade *that* for an ice cream cone?

What we have here is a situation where, if the particular reinforcer didn't work, we might wonder if the promise of an ice cream cone was enough. I believe there will be times when the promise of a Mercedes-Benz will *not* be enough. Unseen payoffs are tremendously powerful.

Here's the good news: If you can account for all the "invisible" payoffs, just about *anything* you put on the plate has a decent chance of working.

(This isn't the first mention of the power of invisible payoffs for inappropriate behavior, nor will it be the last. Unseen and unrecognized payoffs are a major issue in managing poor behavior.)

A skyrocketing ante: What if the youngster keeps pumping up the ante? One downside to offering rewards for performance occurs when a youngster plays *Let's Make a Deal*, wanting *more* goodies for the same compliance. At what point is this hopeful limit-testing on the child's part versus it becoming a juvenile version of extortion?

The thinking part: Is behavior modification cognitive enough? Does it actively engage thinking and reasoning in achieving compliance and change? For years, I thought perhaps I was alone in posing this question. I then attended a program by Dr. Ross Greene, author of *The Explosive Child* (Greene, 1998) and the more recent, *Lost at School* (Greene, 2007). Dr. Greene posed the same question and answered it: "With difficult kids, behavior modification isn't cognitive enough." It addresses behavior, but not thought.

Consider how you could put some one-celled critters on one side of a Petri dish and their favorite food on the other side. What will they do? They will cross the dish and have lunch, right? Is that behavior modification? Yes, it is. And just how cognitive and "smart" do those little guys have to be to get to the food? Answer: They only have to be smart enough to know they're hungry!

What does this mean about using contingency management and reinforcers with children and adolescents who have infinitely more cognitive horsepower than what's floating around in the Petri dish? Young people can *see* through our intent, *examine* our motives, and *decide* whether or not they want to play at all.

Why should we be so surprised when we make an attractive offer and the youngster says or does, "No!"

Use of rewards: Should we even be offering tangible rewards for desired behavior?

In his monthly newsletter, Dr. Marv Marshall, founder of the Raise Responsibility System and author of the books *Discipline without Stress, Rewards, or Punishment* and *Parenting without Stress* (Marshall, 2001 & 2010), told about a school administrator that changed the way students raise funds for the school's charities.

In this school students are not offered rewards, prizes, or incentives for bringing in the most money for the charity. The school didn't want students raising funds motivated only by the tangible benefits they could receive. (Correct me if I'm wrong, but it's not at all unusual for a charity to come to a school assembly and spend more time showing students the prizes they could win than sharing the work and function of the charity. Yes, it's the way to raise the healthiest amount of cash, but what's the message?)

In order to help students understand that doing something good for a worthy charity is its own reward, this school administrator asks the charities to take whatever they would spend on prizes and add it to the donations raised by that school. Yeah, it's a radical approach, perhaps bringing in fewer funds, but it does serve to put things back into an intended perspective.

It's a mistake to expect all young people, especially the youngest ones, to have a complete grasp of the need for benevolence and kindhearted gestures. Most kids really can't identify with or grasp the notion of what it would feel like to go hungry for a few days. Still, it is important to encourage them to act in ways that are noble and selfless, and that the best rewards come from the inside.

What about other values, like kindness, honesty, and caring? Do we stand to cheapen these gestures if we offer material rewards?

Desired rewards: Just because we're fond of a certain reward doesn't mean it will appeal to the youngster. This is especially true with tangible reinforcement. For instance, if someone offered my wife a chocolate milkshake as a reward when she was a child, it wouldn't work. She is highly allergic to chocolate.

In the working world employees often will work harder for a job title or a parking spot than for a raise in salary. We're not all the same, and we don't all want the same things. (Wouldn't it be arrogant on my part to assume I *knew* what everyone wanted?)

As a rule, activities (and opportunities to do those activities) appeal more to young people than tangible incentives. (This is good news because they are also less expensive.) These kinds of incentives could include ten minutes of free time on the computer, or the opportunity to go down to the first grade and help younger students with reading.

A long, long wait: Do we really want to *wait* on behavior modification? The whole premise of behavior modification is incremental changes in behavior over time. But what if we find ways to change some behaviors quickly? Wouldn't that be better than dragging out the change over weeks and months? Chapter Eight will show us just how quickly permanent change can happen.

Selling off of responsibility: One hidden drawback of relying too strongly on behavior modification is that it can shift responsibility for behavioral change from the child onto the adult (or be perceived as such). A frustrated parent or teacher can blame themselves for a youngster's bad behavior, feeling they failed to find the right behavior management "key" to unlock compliance. Moreover, the child can see it the same way, and depend on the adult to change their (the child's) behavior.

What Needs to Happen?

I'm not at all suggesting we toss out all tangible rewards and incentives; they have their place. My wife taught developmentally handicapped youngsters for 14 years. In knowing her students were limited in cognitive and reasoning skills, she emphasized motivators and rewards they could see, experience, and touch. These incentives *needed* to be tangible. But she also knew and understood that authentic change in a youngster's behavior was based more on relationships than any other single factor. The strength of a relationship will trump rewards every time. And that hasn't changed since we were writing on stone tablets.

Emphasize responsibility: My educator friend in California, Dr. Marv Marshall, put this whole behavior modification thing into sharp focus in his email newsletter, "Promoting Responsibility and Learning" (Marshall, 2007). That issue contained the following contribution from an educator. It squarely addresses one of the just-discussed drawbacks of using rewards and incentives to modify behavior. (To subscribe to this excellent newsletter, go to www.marvinmarshall.com.)

One of the oddest conversations I ever had with a child was with a very bright second grader. He had a history of misbehavior at school, with lots of office time and suspensions. At the beginning of the year, I sat with him after a minor infraction and, during our conversation, I casually said something like, "Well, you know I can't MAKE you behave. That's something you'll have to want to do for yourself. You get to think about your behavior and what you do here in the classroom." (Not my exact words, but something like that.)

At this the boy looked at me and said, "But you HAVE to make me behave. That's your job!"

75

We must have spent about 15 minutes in a conversation that ended up centering not only on the misbehavior that had occurred, but on an idea he had somehow picked up from kindergarten and first grade: It was MY job to be in charge of his behavior.

He pointed out that I should or could use behavior charts (he knew of several), or prizes or stickers. He had all sorts of suggestions for me of ways I could change his behavior. It was hysterical, and he was not very pleased initially that I was not interested into buying into any of his stuff.

Needless to say, although it took some time, this child did eventually figure out how to be in charge of his behavior in our classroom. I think and hope the lessons he learned serve him better in the future than his notion of teachers controlling him. But boy, what an eye-opener for what we do to kids with some of our behavior systems.

Hey, there's not much I could add to that. Responsibility for change *must* rest with the youngster.

Appeal to reason: Some kids are unreasonable; that's a given. Most, however, are more willing to comply when the request seems reasonable and fair.

When I was in the service, I was taught to give a reason for a direct order whenever possible. It left the impression of purpose to the order, not just some petty officer spouting off:

> *Smith and Jones, move these six file cabinets to the center of the room. A crew is coming over to paint the bulkheads.*

A parent can do the same thing, and perhaps sweeten the pot in the process:

> *Susan, you've been wanting me to take you fishing. That would be fun, but those tackle boxes are a mess. Everything is one big tangle. If you think you could straighten them out by Saturday, we'll go to the lake.*

Here's another:

> *Todd, you've been wanting to go out and practice your driving, but I need to finish fixing this garbage disposal, then I have to cut the grass. If you'll get started on the yard while I wrap up this job, I think we could work in a little drive time.*

Notice how both of these examples offered an activity (rather than a tangible incentive) the parent *knew* was valuable to Susan and Todd. Plus (and this is a biggie), there was no payoff or inconvenience to others if the youngster *didn't* comply.

A reasonable request doesn't even have to contain a direct pay-off for the youngster:

My goodness; time is slipping away. Grandma will be here in less than an hour and I'm not anywhere near ready. Marty, would you please put these sheets in the washer with one capful of detergent? I'd really appreciate it.

Wouldn't it take Marty more time to avoid the task than simply do it? It pays to set this up with a quick, short task. It also helps if, later, Mom will again, in a quick, reflective comment, express her appreciation to her daughter.

Teachers can find similar opportunities for quick and cooperative compliance to abound in the classroom, also.

Creatively encourage compliance: It's difficult to "buy" a stubborn and difficult kid, regardless of what's on the plate. (I've always said that a much bigger payoff is stuck to the *bottom* of that plate: It's the option of frustrating us, and it's a *huge* payoff.) Here are a few ideas that serve to reduce the size of the plate, or perhaps eliminate the plate entirely.

Offer a choice: Choice always looks better to the youngster because, regardless of what the adult offers, there's an option. Choice is the most basic form of empowerment. It substantially reduces conflict and, in most instances, it works well.

One way to "load" choices is to make one or more of them ridiculously undesirable:

Barbara, I have three chores that need to be done. You can pick one. The bathrooms need to be cleaned, the trash needs to be taken out, and ALL the windows need to be washed. Your choice.

Barbara's smart. She knows she can take out the trash in less than 60 seconds. This strategy succeeds because it gains compliance; period. Besides, the windows were never an issue in the first place. (But they *did* get the trash moved.)

Another "spin" on choice is the parent's offer to take the remaining choice:

Barbara, I have two chores that need to be done. The bathrooms need to be cleaned and the trash needs to be taken out. If you'll pick one and get to it, I'll take the other. What'll it be?

How could a parent be more reasonable and fair than that? If the parent then goes straight to the remaining task, there's subtle pressure on Barbara to do the same with the chore she selected.

The same concept works in the classroom, also. The teacher prepares two or more assignments. One has four problems or questions on the page; the other has 20. The student is instructed to select one assignment and get started.

Another idea on offering choice opens options for beginning and completing the task:

Robert, you can do that chore right now, you can do it in an hour, or you can do it right after dinner. Just let me know what time you decide.

Remember, *any* choice can be empowering.

Provide a discard: A discard is more powerful than a tangible payoff because it immediately reduces the taskload, the issue of the defiance in the first place. In using this strategy with my son, I would set a condition to the discard:

Jamie, I have five chores I need for you to do. If you can finish three of them by five o'clock, you can hand two of them back to me.

Being his mother's child, also, the boy *always* went for the sale. I don't think he ever realized I only wanted him to do *three* chores, not five. But, if I had asked for three chores from the start, there would have been resistance. The solution is in the "packaging."

Suggest a compliance discount: This intervention is a bit different from offering a discard in that the youngster has to demonstrate compliance to earn the payoff. The bottom line is the same: The task is reduced.

This is an easy one to implement at school:

Students, you have your assignment. Notice there are ten problems on the page. I'm going to set two timers to go off. One will go off in the first half of the activity; the other will go off during the second half. If either or both timers catch you in your seat and doing this assignment, you can write "free" next to the problem of your choice.

Students figure it out pretty quickly that if they will simply do their work, there will be less of it to do.

(Note: I recommend a rather "loose" interpretation of compliance in this intervention. If a student is in his seat, is facing the front of the class, and has all his materials in front of him when the timer goes off, that's fine. I don't want to get into a conflict with a student regarding how much he has to demonstrate "doing this assignment." The whole point could get lost in an argument, especially with a difficult student. Think about it: If he's in his seat, is facing the front of the class, and has all his stuff, that's a good day right there!)

This strategy works well at home, also. The parent sets a timer during chore time. If the timer catches the youngster doing an assigned chore, she can return one chore to the parent. (You might want to turn the timer to the wall or cover it with a cloth so the child can't "plan" their compliance as the timer ticks down. Also, consider using random settings each day. That way, there won't be a pattern to it.)

Make 'em think: Sometimes the best reinforcement is one that is not promised at all. You read it correctly; not promised *at all*: It's thinly inferred. What I'm suggesting maximizes reasoning and challenges the expectations of the youngster. In essence, it deals effectively with defiant behavior by removing payoffs for the defiance.

By way of an example, let's say a teacher promises to give each student who finishes their work before class is over an ice cream sandwich at lunch. That's not a bad deal; she'll probably have a few takers.

She already has a pretty good idea what her most defiant student *might* say: "That's okay; I don't like ice cream" or "I'm allergic to dairy products." (That's another downside of offering tangible rewards to defiant youngsters: They can find a way to trash them.)

Here's a better deal, and it will give the teacher more results with a *lot* less effort. She promises them nothing at all. Nothing!

During lunch she's walking around the cafeteria handing out the treats to the three or four students who made the effort to turn in their work before they went to lunch. She whispers to those students why she's giving out the ice cream sandwiches, deliberately making the whole gesture low-key.

Do you think this will get around? Only like wildfire. On the next day there will be students sitting there wondering if the ice cream sandwich deal is "On" or "Off." The teacher, making a little room for them to turn it over in their minds, offers no clear clues. It *might* happen. More students will turn their work in, just in case.

Another teacher offered her students little more than encouragement. It worked well, also. She validated their compliance *before* they started a task. (How's that for a novel approach?)

She would give her students an assignment then, while they still had only their heading on their paper, she would walk through the classroom writing brief comments on no more than three or four papers:

Great job! Good work! Excellent!

She would add her initials with a flourish and continue to walk the aisles looking at papers. It wouldn't be long before her comments on a blank paper would draw a question:

Miss, you just wrote "Great Job!" on my paper!

Yes, I did.

But, I haven't done anything yet.

But didn't you intend to do a great job on that paper?

I did.

There you go. (as she kept walking)

Over the course of a school week, the teacher would write a comment on *every* student's paper.

This little strategy tends to confuse and challenge youngsters, but in a positive way. If they decide *not* to do their work after the teacher writes good comments on their paper, they're pretty sure the comments might stop. To stop or not do the work would be to show defiance in the face of a kind and generous gesture. It would require an "unreasonable" level of defiance that students could not justify easily. Most youngsters wouldn't risk it. Besides, they *like* having the teacher write nice things on their paper. (And, yes, there are those few who have trouble with *positive* comments.)

It's not difficult to use the same idea at home. A parent could praise their child's ability with the chore *before* they do it, or check while the child is doing the chore and make a positive comment about it. The parents could even offer to finish the chore for the child (that would shock the youngster), or they could praise the work by offering the child a coupon for a chore holiday. There are *lots* of possibilities.

A Final Thought

There are those who might say the interventions offered here are actually a type of behavior modification because of the intent of the strategy. No argument there. The purpose of these interventions is to encourage compliance while minimizing the drawbacks of using tangible rewards and incentives.

For additional ideas on generating more compliance with difficult youngsters, go to the library and check out *If My Kid's So Nice, Why's He Driving ME Crazy?*, *101 Ways to Make Your Classroom Special*, and *What Parents Need to Know About ODD* (Sutton, 1997, 1999, and 2007). You can also find these books at www.friendlyoakspublications.com.

Chapter Seven

The "Loop"

Conflict is a by-product of coercion. In relationships, conflict comes when someone uses coercion or force to change the behaviors or habits of others. Although coercion, force, and threat can be effective in the short-term, the conflict generated can do serious damage. Some of this damage can hang around for a long, long time.

Dr. Gerald Patterson of the University of Oregon has spent a big part of his career studying the effects of coercion between individuals. In fact, he developed a term for it: The Coercive Process or The Coercive Loop. (If you ever studied Transactional Analysis, quite popular in the '70s, you likely would be familiar with conflicts and how they develop within communication styles.)

Dr. Patterson has shown us how the course and outcomes of coercive conflict between individuals is amazingly predictable. That's good news, because predictable situations and circumstances can be addressed and changed. As we will see, knowing about predictable elements is paramount to shutting them down.

(I must add here I've never met nor communicated with Dr. Patterson directly. Much of my exposure to his work came from reading and from personal contact with my friend, Ivan Vance, an educational specialist in north Texas. I also learned about Dr. Patterson's work from Dr. Jeremy Shapiro, a clinical psychologist at Case Western Reserve University in Cleveland. The conclusions I draw here, as well as the interventions I suggest, are mine.)

A Scenario of Coercion

It's a common picture. It begins when one person provokes another in some way. The offended party then retaliates, cranking up the intensity a bit. The first person won't stand for that, and comes back with a response certain to contain even more gusto. Neither of them intend to give ground. This situation continues back and forth, becoming more heated and more volatile at each exchange.

As a coercive conflict festers and boils, the issue that started it can get buried in the conflict. With all the negativity the conflict brings, original issues or requests for compliance remain unresolved.

Conflicted and coercive exchanges might seem spontaneous and unique but, according to my understanding of Dr. Patterson's excellent work, these negative interactions predictably culminate in one of two ways: Someone either capitulates and gives in, or someone moves to more drastic measures like physical retaliation or heavy threat. Either way, someone has to lose, and they *don't* like it.

A goal of avoidance: Consider how a bright and defiant youngster might use this loop business to her advantage. If Mom makes a compliance request and the girl knows a prolonged argument will wear her mother down, the argument works to the youngster's benefit. If she can put enough strain on Mom, the girl won't have to do much of anything else.

Postponed permanently: A need to avoid an argument can stop a coercive loop, but at a cost. A parent realizes a conflict is building and says, "It's obvious we can't talk about this right now. We'll deal with it later." It's very possible "later" will never happen. If a youngster knows this is likely to be the case, she can press the conflict enough to cause the parent to postpone the discussion indefinitely (or permanently).

"Feed the Dog!"

Here's an example of a coercive loop. Mom comes in from work and notices that her son's one chore for the afternoon, feeding the dog, isn't done. She walks into the den and there's Jimmy, absorbed in a TV program. Mom is not happy.

> *Jimmy, aren't you supposed to feed the dog as soon as you get home from school ... BEFORE you turn on the television?*

Without as much as looking up, Jimmy mumbles something about doing the chore during the next commercial. Mom leaves.

When she comes back twenty minutes later, the dog *still* hasn't been fed. This time, Mom's upset.

> *I thought you were going to feed the dog during a commercial. What's the deal, Jimmy? FEED THE DOG!*

> *During the next commercial, Mom; I promise.*

Mom's not totally convinced, but she again leaves the room.

Nothing has changed when she comes back later. Now she's *really* upset!

> *If I have to come back again to tell you to feed the dog, I'm getting the belt. Do you hear me, Jimmy?*

When she returns, guess what? The poor dog *still* hasn't been fed. As we have learned, there are one of two endings to the "loop" at this point: capitulation or "Crunch Time" (my terms).

Capitulation: In this ending Mom simply is tired of asking.

Well, SOMEONE has to feed this poor animal!

She feeds the pooch herself. (Jimmy could have been holding out for this one all along. His noncompliance has been effectively rewarded: He never left the TV.)

"Crunch Time:" In another ending Mom indicates she is going for the belt. At the last possible instant, Jimmy makes a move toward the dog's bowl.

Okay, okay, I'm feeding him, Mom.

Jimmy feeds the dog, but *only* after he knows Mom means business. (Of course, there is another possibility: Mom uses the belt on Jimmy. Who knows what happens after that?)

No-win Outcomes

Neither of these outcomes of a coercive loop are really acceptable. Applying threat might bring about some compliance, but it will always be temporary compliance. The only way to get that same compliance next time is to use threat again. This is not exactly the best recipe for a good relationship.

Think about it; Mom has a hard day at work and gets another dose of misery from her son when she gets home. How much time would she *want* to spend with him on this particular evening? Mom and Jimmy could drift further and further apart.

And the dog isn't happy, either.

But the capitulation outcome doesn't fare any better. It closely approximates a pitiful attempt to shame another person into compliance, or worse yet, a surrender prompted by exhaustion. It might have no effect at all, or it might even work a time or two. As a strategy, however, it has a rotten shelf life. Who repeatedly wants to be *shamed* into doing anything?

What Needs to Happen

Breaking out of a coercive loop means shutting down the coercion; period. It means at least one of the two people in the loop needs to exercise enough level-headedness and insight to take the high road. In this instance, Mom needs a better plan.

Breaking out of a coercive loop, or coercive process, requires two things:

> 1. *A genuine relationship.* In the case of interactions with strangers, it would be a sense of social responsibility.
>
> 2. *A strategy for getting the compliance up front.* This means getting the task done the *first* time it's requested. If this were to happen, there would be no coercive process. But that's the whole point, isn't it?

In the example of the mother, the son, and the task of feeding the dog, it's critical for Mom to understand it's much easier to get Jimmy to feed the dog *before* he turns on the television. Any youngster involved in a fun or engaging task doesn't want to leave it.

It's suggested that Mom sit down with Jimmy at a time when there is no problem or conflict. It would also help if this discussion is conducted in a location other than the place where the problem festered. The discussion might go something like this, with Mom opening:

Jimmy I don't like it when we struggle and fight over a chore like feeding the dog. Do you like it when we struggle and fight?

Uh, no.

Do you think it works better for you and for me when we don't struggle and fight ... when I'm NOT getting so upset with you?

I guess so.

I agree, Jimmy; I agree. It's much better in this house when we aren't getting upset with each other. Do you think perhaps we could work at things being better between us and the chores still *getting done?*

Yeah, Mom; but how?

One way might be for you to feed the dog before you even pick up the remote control for the TV. (Laughing) *Why, we could even put the dog's bowl on top of the remote as a reminder. Do you think that would work?*

(Laughing) *That would probably work.*

And if it does work, Jimmy, I'll make you this promise. I will notice when you take care of chores like that on your own without my having to remind you about it over and over again. And I'll bet you'll know that I have noticed, because I'll have a smile on my face when I do it, instead of being angry at you. Would that be a good thing?

That would be a good thing, Mom.

It's hardly my intent to make this a pie-in-the-sky sort of dialog where everything works out perfectly; we all know better. Benefits of this sort of direct and positive dialog, however, can lead to an improved lifestyle and a much-improved relationship.

Let me also add here that, in countless sessions I have had with youngsters, they universally voice regret about how unpleasant circumstances become when they have conflict with their folks. In speaking specifically of the hard feelings and discord that erupt as a by-product of strife, these youngsters share with sincerity how they *don't* like these feelings coming between them and their parents.

What I'm saying here is that our children and students want good relationships with us as much as we do. (Well, *most* of 'em do). It's likely they, too, will be receptive to strategies that cut out the hassle and strife.

We need only point them in the right direction. Chapter Twenty-two will outline a win/win process for avoiding "looped" conflicts altogether. For now, keep in mind that the person who can gain compliance while minimizing coercion will come out on top just about every time.

Part Two

Creating Change

Chapter Eight

Between Heartbeats

There are folks who see behavioral change as a long, slow, midnight train moving somewhere in the darkness. Change comes, perhaps, but one rambling boxcar at a time.

It's not exactly a vision full of excitement and vitality.

Yes, some change, like weight loss, is best done over a period of time, but how quickly does a young child learn that a stovetop is *hot*? One experience can cement permanent, everlasting learning and change. It literally can happen in a heartbeat.

"Belle"

Here's a little story that shows just how quickly behavior can change. It's from *Memphis Belle*, a 1990 Warner Brothers picture. It's the story of the first B-17 bomber and crew to complete 25 missions against Germany and return home. (The real names of the crew were not used in the picture.)

Dennis is the pilot of the bomber; Luke the copilot. These men could not be more different. Dennis is a bit of an introvert, a likeable guy, but serious and all business when it's time to put Belle into the air.

Luke, on the other hand, is an extrovert, always hungry for action. He longs to be a fighter pilot, where he can make all the decisions and be the devil-may-care ace aviator. He resents sitting in what he calls the "Dummy Seat," the copilot's position on Belle. Luke's a good pilot, but his resentment at playing second fiddle on the bomber fuels his defiance toward Dennis.

94

You can sense the tension in the cockpit as they prepare for this their 25th and last bombing run into enemy territory.

Dennis doesn't know Luke has cut a deal with Clay, Belle's tail gunner. Luke wants desperately to shoot down an enemy fighter. With a lot of begging and pleading, he convinces Clay to let him shoot the tail gun during this last mission.

As Belle is under attack by German fighters, Clay, in his pre-arranged scheme with Luke, calls for more ammunition. Luke offers to take it back to him.

Luke climbs into the tail gunner's position and, true to his desire, shoots down an enemy fighter. But, in going down, the wounded fighter slices through the fuselage of a bomber in their B-17 group. The bomber breaks apart and falls from the sky. Only two parachutes are confirmed; eight men die for certain.

Luke can't believe it. He is stunned as he leaves the tail gun and heads back toward Dennis in the cockpit. As he gets back into the copilots's seat, Dennis mentions that he will need Luke's help taking evasive action from the fighters and the flack.

"Anything you say, Dennis," is Luke's reply. "You know what you're doing."

I find Luke's response to Dennis captivating and revealing. In an instant, he was changed from the action-starved aviator to a player who realized the stakes were real, and that he had a responsibility to help get his crew back to England and home safely.

Yes, change *can* happen in a heartbeat.

What Needs to Happen

It's my belief we should stop holding to the notion that change must be a drawn-out objective, and that all change in a youngster's behavior must be systematically altered and improved over an extended period of time. That does not have to be the case.

Luke's behavior changed in seconds. Why? It changed in an instant of epiphany when Luke realized (the hard way) that Dennis had been right all along. As the pilot, Dennis had shouldered enormous responsibility for his men and the mission. Luke, in that moment of epiphany, *voluntarily* surrendered the behaviors that were not appropriate.

Please note: No one had to *tell* him to do so. I also believe the experience changed parts of Luke for the rest of his life.

Are there instances where gradual change *is* the change of choice? Certainly. More importantly, however, change will happen when youngsters convince *themselves* that change is the best thing for them to do.

Chapter Nine

The ONLY Person You Can Change

Most folks have heard the old adage, "You can't change other people; you can only change yourself." It is true, of course. It's been like that for eons, despite the fact that, in times of conflict, the point is ignored.

We (that's a collective "we") continue to put a ton of effort in our attempts to change others. Most of that effort is wasted in the struggle.

Making other people change is hard work. How many folks get married with the not-so-subtle agendum of changing a few select habits of their future spouse? As time goes by, how successful are they in pulling off those changes in their mate? Anyone who favors such a plan need only check out the divorce rate in this country.

In short, efforts to change others while we ourselves remain unchanged *don't* work.

The Birds

My wife and I lived in a mobile home park shortly after we married. (In our case, "mobile home" was a nice way of saying "trailer.") A good-sized tree shaded the spot where I parked my car. My life as a GI-Bill student and newlywed was going pretty well until an army of waxwings invaded that tree.

That's when life became difficult. These little critters took over the tree and dropped the stuff that comes out of birds. In a short time, there was not a square inch of my car that was spared. I was driving a 1968 Poopmobile.

I was *upset*! How dare they trash my car *and* my life like that.

Exercise in frustration: Oh, to settle the score. I shouted at 'em. I banged on trash can lids. I even doused 'em with a water hose. None of it worked. The waxwings continued to pelt my Plymouth, looking to make their point with the village idiot.

I decided if I couldn't get them all to leave the tree, I'd pick 'em off one at a time. I loaded my air rifle, pulled up a lawn chair, and started making them pay!

Correction: I *tried* to make 'em pay. I pounded 'em with pellets, but to no avail. The birds would scatter with every shot, call in reinforcements, and retake the tree.

Frustrating. Midway through my agony one afternoon, my wife brought a glass of iced tea and asked how the bird project was going.

"It's *not* going," I shouted. "There are more of them now than ever!"

"I suspected that," my lovely bride confided. "If I were you, I'd just *move* the car."

Move the car? That was a revelation to me. Moving the car had *never* entered my consciousness. I had focused entirely on the birds changing, only to discover that birds do what birds do. They weren't *about* to change. Change was possible, but it didn't start with the birds.

Whatever the birds in your life, if you're waiting for *them* to change ... well, I wish you luck. If you're making a lot of noise like I did, hoping they will leave, good luck again. Complaining won't work any better than waiting. There's an excellent chance things can change, and we know where it starts.

A Mom Finds Her Daughter

A parent or teacher relationship must exist with a young person before expectations can be made and honored. I'm referring here to expectations that work in *both* directions. If the expectations begin to crowd the relationship, defiance and noncompliance develop as unwanted baggage.

A psychologist in Albuquerque shared with me a vivid example of this exact situation. She was seeing a young girl and her mother in therapy. As academics became more challenging for the girl, Mom coordinated the assignments with the teacher and insisted her daughter spend even more time on her school work.

Things were fine for awhile, then the girl began to resist. Mom held tough. Conflict grew, while the girl's school work suffered. She accomplished *less* in her studies, not more, and her overall mood and behavior deteriorated. That's when Mom took her to the psychologist.

Expectations gone wrong: Dr. Rivera, the psychologist, used a simple diagram (one I had shared while training in Albuquerque) to show the mother how relationships can be eroded when expectations weigh on them heavily. She explained to Mom how, as we begin to expect more and more from our children and students, the expectations consume the relationship. (Figures 9-1 and 9-2 show the effects of appropriate versus inappropriate expectations on an adult and child relationship.)

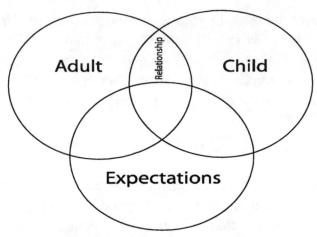

A Balanced Relationship

This diagram shows how the adult and the child have a functioning relationship. Although both of them have expectations of the other, the relationship continues to develop and flourish.

Figure 9-1

It's a simple matter of physics: Two entities cannot occupy the same space at the same time. One of them has to either give way or go away. As the girl "lost" her mother, resentment and hurt fortified her resistance. It became a classic case of noncompliance, victory by default.

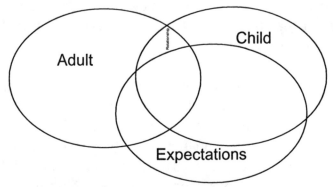

An Unbalanced Relationship

This diagram shows what happens when expectations on the child become excessive. Not only does the child experience the burden of increased expectations, the relationship is affected, also. Defiant behavior is often the child's response in this situation.

Figure 9-2

This particular story has a great ending, as Dr. Rivera wrote:

I used the concept of the overlapping circles with one mother. She is now listening more and judging less, and is being more introspective. Her daughter is finding her way back to school, and is completing homework more readily.

"Come on," some folks might say. "It *can't* be that simple."

Oh, yes; it can.

Kudos to a great mom: The mother Dr. Rivera described was an especially insightful parent. She made a conscious decision in this case to put her daughter *before* her expectations. In doing so, the mother created a change that made a place for their relationship *and* for reasonable expectations.

I'm not at all suggesting we abandon expectations. That would be careless and irresponsible. Relationships between an adult and a young person require expectations of both, but there needs to be room for the relationship to operate and flourish. It's up to the adult to set it up. Just as important, the adult has to *want* to do it.

The Relationship Wrecker (Anger)

It's difficult, bordering on impossible, for a parent or a teacher to rebalance expectations and relationships while they are still angry at the child. They might focus on a strategy, and even see early success with it, only to have it fade in its effectiveness. This is because the youngster quickly learns that an intervention without a relationship feels oppressive. Just like Dr. Rivera's young patient, the child views the adult's actions as little more than trickery.

Who wants to be fed a steady diet of tricks? Anger *must* be addressed before authentic change can happen.

What Needs to Happen?

Obviously, it's important for the adults to start the changes necessary, changes that begin within themselves. It's the willingness to take the high road, to realize that success or failure lies in our capacity and desire to make a shift in our own behavior. Only then can events, circumstances, and others begin to reflect that change.

What does it take to accomplish this? It takes a shift in behavior that starts between our ears. Action can only move on the fuel of insight and positive resolve.

Wedding day changes: My wife and I once stood before someone who had the authority to tell us we were married. At the instant of that announcement, what physical changes took place in us?

None; there were no physical changes at all. What changed in our thoughts and perceptions? Everything. We each made the change from "me" to "we." There was no magic in the minister's words. The magic happened inside each of us. So far, that insight and resolve has lasted over 40 years. (My wife has tremendous tolerance!)

The high road: In taking the high road of deep and personal change, we must also keep foremost in our minds the need to manage our anger and frustration responsibly. Both are a part of our daily lives. We can't avoid them, but we can learn to channel the energy of anger and frustration into the changes we make.

That can be a *lot* of energy!

(As I edited this chapter, it occurred to me that, if folks took it to heart and earnestly began making the changes Dr. Rivera described in the mother, the remainder of this book would simply serve to supplement those changes. Insight and resolve are the doorway to relationship-sustaining change.)

Chapter Ten

Responsibility (and Something Else)

I can still remember clearly the day when, as a school psychologist, I was asked to consult with a seventh-grade math teacher. This man had been put through the mill by a certain 13-year-old.

"I'm tired of trying with that kid," he told me. "Nothing I do works with him. I've tried *everything*!"

"I see," I said. (I wouldn't have wanted him in my classroom either.) "So, uh ... what are you going to do?"

He looked off into space for a moment before he replied. "I'm just going to wait until *he* decides to change his ways."

"You're going to *wait*?"

"Yes! That's *exactly* what I'm going to do. I'm just gonna wait."

I wished him luck, but I wasn't wild about his plan. Waiting as an intervention might work with some situations, but it was a worthless strategy in this case. This 13-year-old boy would have whiskers down to his knees before he ever changed on his own. For this youngster, waiting would be a terrible intervention.

"It's Not My Problem!"

The real message behind "I'm just going to wait" is something closer to, "*He* needs to do the changing, not me." It's another way of putting the whole load on the boy's shoulders and letting it stay right there.

Anyone who has racked up some experience in managing difficult students in the classroom certainly can identify with these exasperating thoughts. But is that always fair? Think about it. If this kid (and a million others) had the slightest clue as to what he could do to perform better in school, experience a measure of peace with his teachers and parents, and have a clear shot at a good day once in a while, wouldn't he have tried it a *long* time ago? And, thinking in purely selfish terms, wouldn't every bit of it have been in his *own* best interest?

I think so. I've met precious few 13-year-olds who *wanted* to overdose on misery.

It's easy to make the mistake of insisting a youngster manage *all* the change. I've made that mistake. Such a position assumes we are certain the youngster knows precisely how he should behave and perform, and deliberately is electing to be difficult and defiant. That could be an enormous mistake. If wrong, a parent or teacher holding to that view would be multiplying the misery for everyone.

(It has been mentioned before, but it's worth repeating: Most specialists are in agreement that chronic bad behavior is the result of poor skills. Good skills aren't going to pop into a youngster's consciousness on their own any more than simply waiting is going to work as a solution to all the problems.)

Exhausting Ignorance

I said, "I've made that mistake," but, from personal experience, I should have known better. In 1966, I went to Navy boot camp in San Diego. (Well, I did have a bit of encouragement from President Johnson.) I had completed junior college, so the company commander designated me as the yeoman for the company. My "extra" job was to assign duties, administer the activities of the company, and keep up with the whereabouts of every man on the roster.

My first report to the battalion headquarters was a disaster. The clerk (to rhyme with "jerk") closest to the door delighted in making misery for anyone just coming aboard. (I found out later he had just finished boot camp himself; he was waiting on his security clearance for a school.)

He proceeded to curse me out, criticizing my reporting procedure. I did not have a clue, and he was not inclined to tell me. The "punishment" for my ignorance was to run downstairs and upstairs through all four company barracks while screaming, "I'm *stupid*; *I'm a dummy!*" Then I was to report to him again. I'm sure he felt a vigorous, humiliating experience would somehow light the fires of knowledge within me, causing the reporting procedure to just pop into my head.

Well, it didn't. After what seemed like dozens of failed attempts to report, each one accompanied by yet another hoarse trip through the companies, I was exhausted. Burial at sea was starting to look pretty good.

Finally, a kind-faced chief (chief petty officer) took pity on me. He pulled me aside and taught me the magic words, the reporting protocol: "Sutton, J.D., B70-45-77, Company 426, reporting as ordered." (A gesture of respect would be added at the end if an officer was being addressed.)

"That's better," the clerk mumbled, as he accepted my report. That day I made a decision I would carry with me for the rest of my life: This world contains both clerks and chiefs. That day I knew which one I wanted to be.

Not My Fault, But My Job

This brings us back to the adults in the 13-year-old boy's life, especially those who are willing to do *something* to jump-start this youngster into a better direction.

Just imagine Johnny's dad lays into the boy for breaking some bottles in the garage. After a pretty rough time with the old man, he climbs on the school bus. Imagine, also, you're his first teacher for the day. He's upset as he walks into your classroom, still choking on some really raw feelings.

In no way are these before-school circumstances your fault. How it plays out in your classroom, however, becomes your responsibility. It might not be fair, but there it is, in your lap.

This stuff happens all the time. (And what about the reverse of the situation, where Johnny comes home upset following an incident at school.) Although waiting might be a short-term option, if Johnny is steamed enough to clock the first person who crosses him, you'd better do *something*. (In some instances, it might be a case of what you *shouldn't* do.)

Something Else: "Want to"

Teachers and parents differ considerably in their willingness to make themselves a resource to an acting-out son, daughter, or student. (In writing this I realize I've been on both ends of that continuum, and all points in between.) The way some youngsters act out only widens the gap.

It's not at all easy or comfortable to exercise responsibility with a youngster who seems dead-set on being totally unreasonable. Unfortunately, the anger and bitterness of the adult only serve to shift this kid's behavior into a higher gear. We've all experienced it.

Question: Has throwing gasoline on a fire *ever* put it out?

Next question: *Why* do we keep doing it?

Frank Bird, my educator friend in Georgia, moved the whole issue of taking responsibility for what enters the classroom straight to the bottom line. He was talking about teachers, but it certainly applies to parents, also.

"They have to *want* to do it," Frank said. Now that hits the target squarely, doesn't it? It's always been interesting to me how we can teach youngsters any number of skills, yet the approaches for teaching "want to" seem so elusive.

The million-dollar question: As an example, all of us are plenty smart enough to become millionaires. That's a fact. It doesn't take a ton of brains to achieve it (although brains are a plus), but it does take a boatload of gumption, a fire in the belly. No fire, no self-made millionaire.

If you ask a roomful of people how many of them would like to become millionaires, most would raise their hands. But precious few would ever commit to focusing that desire into a bank account reality. Perhaps a few folks will buy the "how-to" books, but few will ever finish even one of them.

But wasn't that the problem all along? They can't even finish a book. What does that mean?

Frank, you're absolutely right. "Want to" is often the whole point.

Contagious "want to:" Those who do have the desire to accomplish something significant, plus a plan for directing and focusing that energy, can leave the rest of us in the dust. As teachers, they can grow fruit on the Tree of Apathy. Kids will follow them, just like they followed Jaime Escalante (*Stand and Deliver*, 1998), Glen Holland (*Mr. Holland's Opus*, 1995), Roberta Guaspari (*Music of the Heart*, 1999), and Ron Clark (*The Ron Clark Story*, 2006). Our young people today are starving for adults with "want to," folks like these, to walk into their lives.

108

What Needs to Happen?

The process of figuring out why a youngster is being behaviorally inappropriate or noncompliant isn't rocket science, but it does require some direction and effort on the part of key adults.

Documenting the difficulty: Current federal guidelines for educators require teachers to develop, implement, document, and evaluate alternative interventions with any student presenting behavioral or academic difficulty. This must be done before a referral for assessment and consideration for Special Education placement and programming can be made.

This has changed the rules in the schools. No longer could the math teacher of the 13-year-old boy tell me he had tried every intervention to fix the issues, then pass the boy over to Special Education for assessment and possible placement. He would first need to present his documentation showing the interventions he had tried and their results.

The whole point of stressing documentation, of course, is that there is the strong possibility one or several interventions will solve the problem without removing the student from the classroom for special instruction and intervention. (It also keeps a youngster from carrying the "label" of a handicapping condition or disability.)

Has this emphasis on responsibility in trying different approaches and documenting them made a difference? The answer is a resounding, "Yes!" I have the opportunity to visit with Special Education directors and supervisors all over the country. They tell me that success in the early tiers of intervention has cut Special Education referrals in *half*.

That's great news, isn't it? When implemented effectively, this philosophy runs even deeper: It represents a success for a teacher that can be replicated with other students, adding to that teacher's confidence, along with a full toolbox of ideas and strategies that have worked.

Back to the 13-year-old: What would I do if I were the math teacher of the 7th-grade student we've been considering through this chapter? I would pose some questions, then build my interventions around them. (Parents: Although this is a school environment, I would pose similar questions for the home as well.)

1. *What is the problem exactly?* Can we isolate it? This might be much easier said than done, but I'd attempt to determine if the primary issues with the student are mostly behavioral or academic. Do the test scores indicate a youngster's ability to handle the academics? If it seems to be academic and content-related, specifically what sort of problem does the youngster present? Do academic difficulties spill over into behavior, especially avoidant behavior? Is there a "collection" of disciplinary referrals already? When and where do behavior problems most often occur? Could these circumstances be altered in any way that would improve outcomes?

2. *How pervasive is the problem?* Is the problem active and ongoing all the time, or is it hit or miss? Do there appear to be any triggers that set off the problem behavior? Are there any variables that could possibly be "tweaked" by intervention? Is the youngster having difficulty in my class only, or in all or most of his classes? If it's just happening in *my* class, what does that mean? What could I do to redirect the behavior or the student's resistance?

3. *Does the problem involve peers?* Peer involvement could make a problem worse or it could be a solution. Youngsters don't always have the skills to get along with peers effectively. If this is a factor, how might it be addressed? Could I use pairings or small groups to help this student academically?

4. *What is the student's overall mood?* This would tell me a lot. Does the youngster always look irritated and upset? Does he seem to be predominately sad-faced? Does he seem resigned to things as they are? Conversely, are there times when the student is more cheerful and positive? On balance, how is mood expressed across a school week? (I would chart it, especially when I prepare to visit with the student about his behavior and performance.) Is the youngster ill and absent a lot? Does the school nurse have any information that might help?

(I remember a situation in which a student was completely deaf in one ear. She had been seated with her best ear to the wall. When the teacher became aware of the situation and changed the seating, all difficulty with that student evaporated. Sometimes solutions are just that simple.)

Karen Ledet, a teacher in Vernon, Florida, uses what she calls The Privacy Desk. One or several desks are set up along the walls of the classroom, out of the rows and columns that are so typical. Any student wanting a bit more space on a given day (can't concentrate, is irritable, doesn't want to be so close to annoying classmates, etc.) simply can move to one of the privacy desks. Sometimes they stay there for the whole class, sometimes not, but Karen shares how students appreciate having this option available. (It's always presented as an option, *never* a consequence.)

5. *How receptive is the student to assistance and intervention?* Not all students are open to help, especially if it comes from the teacher while class is going on. Some kids see help from the teacher as an embarrassment. Could I work around this issue, or perhaps use a screen in a way that peers don't see how this youngster struggles with reading, for instance? The opportunity for this student to work with others in a small group can change the dynamics a great deal. Would this student feel better about help from a peer instead of from me? Could I pair them on a project, allowing this youngster to bask in the positive light of a successful experience? What could be the long-term benefits of that?

6. *How do the parents see the problem?* I would never know if I didn't ask. Parents have known this child for many years; they are clued in to the youngster's habits and behaviors. They might have excellent feedback as to what's happening and how best to address it. I would also want to know about any changes in the youngster's home life, such as a military parent deploying or loss of a grandparent. These circumstances can have a profound effect on a student's behavior and capacity to concentrate.

7. *What does the student think?* Will he talk to me, or does he just shrug his shoulders? Do I believe he sees me as a resource or an obstacle? (It matters

greatly.) Can I improve in my ability to reach out to him over time? Will he help me help him with interventions?

Obviously, these questions and thoughts don't cover everything, but they are a start as I consider ways to develop, implement, document, and evaluate interventions for overcoming behavioral and academic issues.

On the floor, and in your face: It's not always a matter of what we do, but rather what we *don't do* when difficulty comes. Here's an example of a fairly common event for a teacher.

The scene: The teacher passes out an assignment to the class. They are to work on it for the remainder of the period. One student glances at it, then wads it into a ball.

"I'm not doing this stupid stuff," he exclaims, as he tosses the wad to the floor.

Hmm, the moment of truth. What does a teacher do? Or, in turning the task a bit, what does a parent do? If the student is already upset, a coercive response could send the youngster right over the edge.

He's *already* in trouble. What else does he have to lose? I know of situations where this sort of exchange escalated into a three-day suspension. And *all* of it could have been avoided.

What should the teacher do? This isn't a pleasant experience for anyone and, if it ever happened to you in the classroom, it *feels* personal, even when it's not. It does help to get a grasp on the notion that a youngster might have a bit more on his plate than the assigned task placed in front of him.

113

The best response I ever heard to the provocative gesture of a paper wadded up and thrown on the floor was powerful in its simplicity. (Aren't the best interventions simple?) Initially, the teacher did nothing. She left the wadded paper on the floor as she helped the class get started on the task.

(The rationale here is to let some time pass, as it disrupts the youngster's intent if the action was a specific gesture to pull the teacher into a conflict. It also allows some opportunity for the student to reconsider, perhaps even to retrieve the assignment from the floor and work on it.)

Eventually, the teacher picked up the assignment, smoothed it out, and placed it and another, fresh copy on the student's desk. She then whispered to the youngster.

"I would appreciate it if, in a little while, you'd drop one of those in the trash can." Then she moved on and gave the boy some space and a chance to comply.

Obviously, there's no guarantee of the student's response, but this teacher could not have made a redirection to task any easier for the both of them. And I'm guessing the student *knew* that. In this redirection the youngster doesn't have to *say* a thing. How good is that, especially if he's still upset? His compliance is verified with a gesture (a quick trip to the trash can), and he can even decide when to do it.

Paying the "want to" price: Before we wrap up this chapter, let's look again at this issue of "want to" on the part of a teacher or parent. It is a powerful component to successful resolution of problems and difficulty at school and home.

I was in Louisiana doing teacher training for St. John's Parish Schools. I had the opportunity to hear Ron Clark deliver an awesome keynote address to the educators gathered there. (Ron Clark is a North Carolina boy, the teacher about whom the film, *The Ron Clark Story* [2006], was made. He was played by actor Matthew Perry. It's a compelling story about Clark's work with challenging students and circumstances in New York City's Harlem.)

During his presentation, Ron shared a story about an effort he once made to encourage students to pay closer attention in class. He told how he entered the class with a large ice chest and challenged them that, for every two minutes he had their undivided attention, he would chug a whole lunch carton of chocolate milk. (He assured them that, if they *did* pay attention, he would most likely throw up at some point.)

The plan worked; he had their *complete* attention. Ron shared how he made it through 14 cartons before ... well, you know.

What happened next, however, was something he had not anticipated. That evening, these students gave their folks an account of what had happened in class. Ron began hearing from parents. They told him that, if he was willing to make himself sick to hold their child's attention in class and help them do better in their schooling and grades, he had their complete support.

I thought about his story on the way home. It poses an interesting question to any teacher or parent:

> *How would most youngsters respond if we were willing to pay the price to reach them?*

Ron Clark charged my battery, that's for sure. His "want to" and efforts to challenge youngsters to a lifetime of achievement continue through his school in Atlanta, The Ron Clark Academy.

I wonder if he lets them serve chocolate milk?

Chapter Eleven

The Miracle Mold

I am now going to share with you a concept that is so far-reaching in its potential for creating powerful positive change you will find it difficult to conceptualize, let alone believe.

I certainly did.

While participating in a convention of the National Speakers Association a few years back, I attended a general session and a breakout session by best-selling author Dr. Joe Vitale. (I discovered he lives not far from me.) In his program, he referenced the work of Hawaiian psychologist, Dr. Ihaleakala Hew Len. To me, Dr. Hew Len pulled off nothing short of a miracle of healing.

An Impossible Task

Dr. Hew Len had what most folks would consider an impossible situation. He was the psychologist for a state hospital ward full of criminally insane patients. Many of these patients wore wrist and ankle restraints. To say these patients were difficult would be a serious understatement. No one wanted to work in that ward; the turnover in staff was nonstop.

He knew it would not be productive to work with these patients in the same way his predecessors did, so Dr. Hew Len altered his focus. He instead worked on himself.

Dr. Hew Len engaged in a process he calls "cleaning." It is derived from the ancient Hawaiian practice of Ho'oponopono. Briefly stated, Ho'oponopono is the practice of responsibility combined with deep sensitivity and humility, as evidenced through thoughts and actions toward others. In a sincere and authentic fashion, these are expressed toward the individual of focus. It is my understanding Dr. Hew Len offered the following in his office while holding each patient's chart:

1. A statement of caring about the patient.

2. An apology to the patient for any thoughts, attitudes, or behaviors that existed between him and that patient.

3. A desire for forgiveness from the patient for those thoughts, attitudes, or behaviors.

4. An expression of gratitude and appreciation to the patient.

This "cleaning," a removal of interpersonal limits, was accomplished with minimal direct contact with the patient.

As Dr. Hew Len worked on himself in removing limits, patients began to heal. Fewer and fewer restraints were needed. Patients became calmer and more content. They spent more time outdoors. Family visits became more rich and meaningful. Staff began to stay and expressed more satisfaction with their work.

The ward was eventually closed. (I will mention shortly how these changes were verified.)

Hearing this in person from Dr. Vitale caused me to consider how this same approach would work with young people. In fact, I became so obsessed with this approach to improvement and healing, I benefited little from the remainder of that convention. I was busy bringing together the very core of this book.

Removing Limits?

Why would changing the behavior of young people for the better need to be difficult? If I made an authentic attempt to remove limits that existed between me and any youngster, shouldn't that result in some kind of change?

But what limits are we talking about? It's a question that has as many answers as there are people asking because, although limits might start in the behavior and appearance of others, it's our own perception that actually creates them. These limits then become a barrier to communication and to the relationship. Too many limits can turn a barrier into a wall that cannot be penetrated with common tools. (What about the limits the math teacher imposed on the 13-year-old student in the last chapter? Is it possible those limits could seal him off from *ever* being effective with that student?)

If a single limit were to interfere with my ability to reach a youngster, just think of the potential for damage done. Here are a few examples of how limits get started:

Situation: A child smells and comes to school poorly dressed.

Limit: "Only an irresponsible parent would send a child to school that way."

Behavior: A student is angry and disrespectful.

Limit: "She just hates ME, that's all!"

Situation: The school psychologist suggests a different intervention.

Limit: "I am exhausted already; how can I work any HARDER?"

Behavior: An adolescent becomes defensive and raises her voice.

Limit: "All you EVER do is scream at me."

Situation: A child becomes ill.

Limit: "The last thing I need is another doctor bill."

Behavior: A youngster won't get out of bed in the morning.

Limit: "Things are tough enough in the mornings around here without you making it MORE difficult for me."

Behavior: A youngster doesn't take out the trash.

Limit: "You don't care to help out around here even a little."

Behavior: A student starts a fight with a classmate.

Limit: "That kid is just plain MEAN."

Situation: Something overheard in the teacher's lounge.

Limit: "Oh no! I'm going to have that student next year."

Behavior: A youngster is defiant and uncooperative.

Limit: "He delights in KEEPING me angry and upset."

Situation: A youngster brings home a friend of questionable reputation.

Limit: "My daughter hangs out with losers."

Situation: Torn school clothes.

Limit: "How careless. Do you think I'm MADE of money?"

Behavior: A student is being especially difficult.

Limit: "This kid just doesn't WANT to change."

Behavior: A child is critical.

Limit: "There's just no way to please you."

Situation: A child wants to live with the other parent.

Limit: "Hey, it's no picnic living with YOU, either."

Dr. Vitale is an established, successful author. I sensed he put his reputation on the line in sharing Dr. Hew Len's story. In the book he coauthored with Dr. Hew Len, *Zero Limits* (Wiley & Sons, 2007), Dr. Vitale shares how he verified Dr. Hew Len's story with records of changes and patient dismissals plus, of course, interviews with staff members who were there and experienced the changes first-hand.

There will be skeptics, of course, just as there are folks who refuse to believe what they can't fully grasp as it comes straight from the box. Complete understanding and the smallest sliver of faith can be miles apart. But I do believe there's something to this business of doing what I can to remove the limits that can fester between a young person and me.

Changed behavior, regardless of how you choose to explain it, is *still* changed behavior.

A Head Start

I reflected on my toughest cases over the years, those children and adolescents who seemed unstoppable in their deviant behaviors. How many of them would have been classified as criminally insane?

Let me see, it was about ... *zero*! I have *never* worked with a youngster who was criminally insane (yet). I had a huge head start on Dr. Hew Len and, for years, I didn't know it.

It's easy to blame a youngster for all the problems, distractions, and disruptions they leave in their wake. I know; I've done it. But I cannot recall a single instance where placing blame created any positive change at all.

It's only when we change *ourselves* that others (especially the young folks we serve every day) can best reflect it back to us. It's a much tougher job than blaming, but the benefits are sitting there waiting on us.

Dr. Hew Len shares that one of his mentors kept a placard on her desk: *Peace begins with me.* It was a statement of profound responsibility and action. What would it be like if everyone took personal action on a statement like that?

What Needs to Happen?

I'm sure there are people who simply cannot fathom that Dr. Hew Len could accomplish what he did, especially in the way he did it. But, in light of his story, consider this: What if the *only* person changed was Dr. Hew Len? Would that change somehow begin to influence others? Mother Teresa didn't always work with cheerful, pleasant patients in Calcutta, but I'm convinced she touched them all for the better. Her change became *their* change.

We don't work with the criminally insane (fortunately). We work with young people who can, by far, more readily receive and return to us the products of change.

Making the shift: Changes that come with the removal of limits may be subtle, but that doesn't reduce their effectiveness over time. It all starts with a shift in how we view a problem or concern, something that has been called a "paradigm shift" in other fields of study. That shift has the power to reduce and remove limits.

Let's revisit some limits and "clean" them with a shift:

Situation: A child smells and comes to school poorly dressed.

Limit: "Only an irresponsible parent would send a child to school that way."

Shift: "Things are likely difficult at home. I wonder if there's something I could do to help?"

Situation: A child becomes ill.

Limit: "The last thing I need is another doctor bill."

Shift: "Susan didn't plan to become sick any more than my checkbook planned to take a hit. We'll make it through, somehow."

Behavior: A student is angry and disrespectful.

Limit: "She just hates ME, that's all!"

Shift: "It's so easy to take these behaviors personally. It's possible they have less to do with me than I think."

Situation: Something overheard in the teacher's lounge.

Limit: "Oh no! I'm going to have that student next year."

Shift: "I can work on that. There's no law that says I *have* to have difficulty with that student."

If changes in my thinking and perception begin to temper how I treat and relate to others, wouldn't they in turn reflect at least a bit of those changes? This sort of change *must* begin with us, the adults. We are more than capable of getting our ship off the rocks, and we are more capable of reducing those limits. No excuses; no passing the buck; no "It's *not* my job."

It *is* my job. It begins with me. Period.

Chapter Twelve

Putting it to Work:
"I Care About You"

So, where are you right now with all this "It begins with *me*" business? Affirmed? Surprised? Discouraged? Thoughtful? Apprehensive? Hopeful? Confused? Encouraged?

All of the above?

Consider again the advantage you have at this point. Dr. Hew Len *couldn't* communicate with his patients much at all; there are reasons why folks are diagnosed as criminally insane. But you *can* communicate. Most all those avenues are open to you. This is in addition to the work you do improving yourself.

That is a tremendous advantage.

"I Care About You"

Of course, we can say, "I care about you," but do we always demonstrate it? Doctors Hew Len and Vitale actually used the words, "I love you." Dr. Hew Len reportedly said it about each criminally insane patient in the ward as he held their chart. He reflected on each patient with love for the essence of humanity clinging to that patient's core.

Whenever we express love or caring about a youngster, it shows up in our actions for and about that young person. How could it not?

A memory revisited: Years ago a couple brought their 15-year-old son to me for evaluation and treatment. The boy was in more trouble than he could handle. There were problems involving drugs, severe behavior issues at school, and episodes of running away from home for days at a time. He was so out of control he eventually had to be hospitalized.

The parents were sick with concern, and they were plenty angry at their son. In taking a history on the young man, I asked his parents to describe the day they brought the boy home from the adoption agency.

"He was such a tiny thing," Mom said. She laughed, surprising herself in the moment. "I think there were more blankets than baby in that package."

She paused for a moment, as if searching for a thought.

"Do you remember our home movie of him right after he learned to walk, the one we took at Easter?" she asked her husband.

"He was all decked out for Easter, bowtie and everything," she continued, with obvious joy in her face and gestures.

"When he got to the end of the sidewalk, he spied this mud puddle. Before we could stop him, he landed in the puddle with both feet. Splash!

"What a mess!" Mom continued. "But what a memory. What a *wonderful* memory."

A mother's anger toward her son was, for a short time, replaced with feelings that had been shuffled to the bottom of the relationship. On the next visit she related with some surprise how her memories of a tiny baby in a bunch of blankets and an old movie of a bowtied toddler in a mud puddle carried her through several evenings of no conflict at home.

My visit with that couple and their son happened more than 20 years before I heard of Dr. Hew Len's experiences with the criminally insane patients. We do tend to relate to others in tandem with our thoughts and feelings about them.

Protective Support

Nothing transmits caring quicker and stronger than our willingness to take action to lift up a child or teen, especially when we don't have to do it.

A trip to the doctor: My father grew up during the depression; money was tight. Sick or injured children got a whole menu of down-on-the-farm remedies before they went to the doctor. (And most of 'em worked!)

I experienced a strong contrast to this philosophy when I became a consultant to a children's home in south Texas. It seemed whenever a youngster there had as much as a sore throat, the facility nurse would take the child into town to see the doctor.

"Are all those doctors' visits *that* necessary?" I asked one of the administrators.

"Probably not," he smiled, "but it's our way of saying we really *want* to take good care of them while they're with us. Putting some feet to that message is more than worth the cost."

He absolutely was correct, wasn't he? It's a simple fact we give better treatment to the people and things we value. Don't our children sense this intuitively?

A bad day in junior high: My wife, Bobbie, deeply admired her father. He was the sort of man who loved his children dearly and wasn't hesitant to put it on the line for them. His favorite admonishment to his children was, "Show me; don't tell me." He used it a lot, but he also practiced it.

Bobbie was an office assistant for one class in junior high school. One day the principal returned to the office and asked if there were any messages.

"No, sir," she replied. "Sir, if there had been any messages for you, I would have told you about them."

He lost it and accused her of talking back to him. While she was still in shock over his tirade, the principal grabbed his paddle and used it on her.

She couldn't believe what was happening. The school nurse, being in earshot of the whole scene, charged into the principal's office and escorted Bobbie to her office. She then picked up the phone and called the house to explain the situation to Bobbie's mother.

While she was sitting in the nurse's office attempting to re-cover from what she later would describe as her worst day in school ever, Bobbie saw her father coming down the hall. (He was a big man; difficult to miss.)

She wasn't sure at first how to interpret his visit to the school. The children had always been told that, if they got into trouble at school, there'd be *more* trouble when they got home.

Her father made sure his daughter was alright, then had a little closed-door "chat" with the principal. He took his daughter home ... after a stop at the local ice cream place. Nothing more was ever said about the incident, but it continued to be yet one more example of how the man didn't have to tell others how much he loved his children. He showed it.

Our actions of caring and support transmit more powerfully than anything we could ever express verbally, although it's still important to say it.

Schedule change: Here's yet another example of the power of caring action on the part of the adult. As a consulting psychologist to a residential treatment center, I worked with one young lady scheduled to go into high school in the fall. She shared her schedule with me one afternoon, noting that she was disappointed the counselor had placed her into a remedial-type freshman English class.

"My language skills *aren't* my problem, Dr. Sutton," she said. (She was right on that. She would often send me the most depressing notes you could imagine, notes that went on and on and on. But they were always grammatically perfect.)

I called the school the next morning and spoke to the counselor. I made a convincing case for the girl's schedule to be changed to a more challenging English class. The change was made and the counselor added she would send for the girl and explain the change to her. The whole conversation lasted less than five minutes.

Later that afternoon the girl saw me in the cafeteria at the facility. She ran up to me and threw her arms around my waist.

"I can trust you now," she exclaimed, as she continued to squeeze. She was happy, and all it took to make it happen was a brief phone call. Just a phone call. It's interesting, too, how a simple act like that opened her trust.

Active Presence

The simple fact that we are physically present with a child transmits our love and caring in a subtle but powerful way.

Bedtime bonding: A parent can sit at the foot of the bed as their son or daughter prepares to go to sleep. (This gesture is not recommended if, for any reason, the child is fearful of that parent.) It can be a silent presence that lasts for only a moment or two, or it can be a gesture that sparks heartfelt dialog. I always suggest the parent let the child take the lead on any dialog that occurs. If they want to talk, fine; if they don't, that's fine, also. Either way, it affirms the youngster and deepens the relationship.

This bedtime presence idea works well because it is done at a time and place that come just moments before an evening's sleep and rest. Since the issues for the day are complete (or as settled as they are going to be), there aren't any detours, distractions, or issues to take away from these moments. Both the parent and child can be more relaxed and spontaneous. It's as close as a parent will get to communication built on the best relationship they can have with their child.

Random acts of sitting: The spontaneous activity of taking a moment to sit with a son, daughter, or student can pay off powerfully. It's different from bedtime bonding in that it can happen anywhere, anytime.

Let's say Junior is playing a video game in the living room. While passing through, Mom makes it a point to sit next to him for a moment, just to watch. Perhaps she makes a comment, perhaps not, but he knows she's there. Then in another moment, she leaves.

Don't underestimate the power of this gesture coming from a parent or teacher. It says simply, "You are worth a moment of my time; no strings attached." When doctors do it well it's called "bedside manner."

While writing this I thought of a similar encounter I had with my grandson several years ago. He couldn't have been more than four or so at the time. He was stretched out on the carpet in our home, watching television.

131

I got down on the floor beside him and stayed there a bit.

"You're a good boy, Jake," I said to him. (It just rolled out of my mouth. I had not planned to say it.)

Jake slowly turned onto his side and looked back at me with a wide smile.

"Thanks, Pop." Then he turned back to his program. That was it. The whole encounter took only seconds, but I felt it communicated volumes.

Wheelin' it: I'm a fan of visiting with a youngster while traveling in the car. It affords the opportunity of a "captive" audience. Where are they going to go? And, from the viewpoint of the driver, this intervention doesn't even require eye contact; natural moments of silence can be absorbed by the passing scenery. Those are two huge benefits that make a conversation with the youngster much more comfortable than it might be in other environments.

A co-therapist and I used to do what we called "Cruise Therapy" with youngsters in residential treatment. We'd pile 'em all into the facility's van and take off with no particular plan in mind other than the trip itself. We didn't do it all that often, but it always paid off for everyone involved.

One iron-clad rule for visiting while taking a ride is no earphones (or earbuds), music, radio, or any other distractions. If you make that a rule up front it can save a ton of grief. This rule can be approached in a way that even validates rather than annoys the youngster:

Sarah, I look forward to visiting with you when we go to Grandma's Saturday. We don't seem to make enough time for that. Being with you, and what you have to share, is so important to me I don't want either of us to be distracted from it. So I'm not going to sing, juggle, do crossword puzzles or video games, or even listen to the radio. You are special to me, and are much more important than all that stuff. You will have all my attention, Sarah, all of it. And I hope you'll do the same for me. Would that be okay?

Although that's a pretty direct approach, I've had a lot of success with it. As a therapist, however, I've sometimes neglected to use it. It is surprisingly simple and effective.

(As a side note, current research indicates that youngsters, to their detriment, are overly stimulated today. They might initially be uncomfortable with a trip that contains only verbal interaction, but they will, in time, look forward to it as a relief of sorts. It's sort of like going camping, but without getting out of the car.)

Like a big boy: Jimmy, a five-year-old patient of mine, had the attention span of a mosquito. He would walk into my office and immediately start rifling through the toys and games on my bookshelf.

I already wasn't in the best of moods on one of those days. I pointed to a chair by the window.

You know what, Jimmy? I'd like for you to have a seat right there so I can visit with you like a BIG boy.

"Okay," he exclaimed, as he crawled up into the chair.

It worked! All I had to do that morning to get his attention and cooperation was to ask for it. How's *that* for a novel approach?

Affirmations

Young people *want* the approval and affirmation of adults they consider significant in their lives. Even the child who says, "I don't care if anyone likes me," probably *does* care.

(For certain, there are a few youngsters who are socially "disconnected" to the point they might not care, but those are the kids you find in books of emotional and behavioral codes of serious diagnoses. Even then, some of them eventually can be reached.)

Children and adolescents who need affirmation the most likely won't ask for it. They're afraid of being rejected, so they emotionally "hover" somewhere between a growing need and a lingering fear.

But there is a solution. These youngsters are more than willing to respond to the adult who makes the first affirming gesture toward them. It doesn't have to be a large gesture; a touch, a smile, and a kind word will do. Teachers will tell you these are the students who will stop by their classrooms after school for a second helping. These are also the kids who will walk all the way across the grocery store simply to speak with that teacher for a moment.

At home and at school, young people respond to the adults who reach out to them. Let's look at a few ways of creating and delivering affirmations that say, "I care about you" ("I love you").

Noncritical Noticing: I discussed Noncritical Noticing in my book, *What Parents Need to Know About ODD* (Sutton, 2007). It's a great approach to use with any youngster, but it's an especially good one to employ with a child who senses adult affirmations always come with a "catch." (An affirmation with a catch wouldn't be an affirmation at all, would it? An example might be, "I love you ... when you're *good!*")

Noncritical Noticing affirms the presence and even the work of a son, daughter, or student without judging it, thus eliminating the "catch." Frankly, this is not easy to do, as adults tend to be in an evaluation mode with youngsters much of the time. Here are a few examples of how Noncritical Noticing could be implemented:

> *Tommy, I noticed when you finished the model of the jet fighter you were building, you cleared a place for it on your dresser.*

(This comment infers Tommy must have been proud of his work on the model, but it lets him draw that conclusion. See how powerful it could be as an intervention?)

> *Sarah, I see you're using a lot of green in your picture there.*

(Again there's no comment at all as to the significance or meaning of all that green color, only that it was noticed.)

> *Terri, I noticed you put your school backpack on top of your shoes.*

(With no word as to judgement or interpretation, Terri might be pleased you noticed her way of remembering to take her backpack to school.)

*Rodney, when you cut the grass this morning,
I noticed how you used the edger before you
mowed.*

(Although edging before or after mowing might not be that much an issue, Rodney probably appreciates how his efforts were noticed.)

One of the things I really like about Noncritical Noticing is the fact that it empowers a youngster's capacity to employ strategies and make decisions without our interference. Fast-forward the effects of such an approach into the World of Work ten or fifteen years down the road, and you'll find an employee who can be assigned a task and trusted to accomplish it without much supervision at all. That's a skill that can be hauled to the bank.

Noteworthy: I heard about a teacher who made it to a point to say "I care about you" to her students by writing encouragements to them on small sticky notes. She made it a point to do this consistently, but without overdoing it. A little story she told reinforced to me just how this gesture was received:

School was coming to a close; students had turned in their textbooks. I was checking the books for damage, and was removing any papers or items that had been left in them. One of the textbooks gave my heart quite a tug. One student had taken every note I had given her during the year, and had stored them neatly in the back of the textbook.

This is not an isolated story. Kids often will keep encouraging and affirming notes and letters shared with them by caring teachers and parents. Notes like these have permanence. Youngsters can read and reread them as often as the want. But be careful! Notes with negative comments also have permanence.

(I was a struggling GI-Bill student when my wife and I married. I commuted 80 miles round-trip to the university daily, with an evening class or two in my schedule for the week. It made for some long days. My wife would pack my lunch so we could save a few bucks. She would slip little notes of encouragement to me in my lunch sack. Believe me, I always seemed to find one when I most needed it.)

Popsicle sticks: Here's an interesting "I care about you" intervention published in my book for educators, *101 Ways to Make Your Classroom Special* (Sutton, 1999). A teacher wrote students' names on Popsicle sticks, one name per stick. She would then place the whole bunch of sticks into one pocket of her skirt as the school day started.

As the day went by, she casually would select a stick from the pocket, then focus on a specific way to affirm that student. The gesture didn't have to be a lot in terms of intervention, perhaps no more than a silent touch on the student's shoulder, but it was a deliberate affirmation. Her goal was, by the end of the school day, to have transferred all the sticks from one pocket to the other.

This was a great and welcomed intervention, and it took precious little extra effort. There are many ways to "spin" it; be creative!

"On my mind" reminders: This affirmation begins when the youngster is not even present physically. The fact that Sarah is on Dad's mind when she's not with him is precisely what makes this intervention so powerful.

Let's say Dad's on a business trip when he sees some butterfly stationery in the hotel gift shop. He knows Sarah loves anything with butterflies on it. He buys the stationery for his daughter. Back home, he hands her the package from the gift shop.

> *I got this while on my trip, Sarah. You'll never guess who I thought of when I saw it.*

Here's an example where the cost of a small gift is peanuts compared to the value added to the relationship. Sarah knows for certain she was on her father's mind, although there had been hundreds of miles between them at the time. How could you ever place a value on that?

Keep in mind that this "I care about you" intevention doesn't have to require any cost or expense at all. I once read an article about a national shortage of chefs in an inflight magazine. At the time, I was working with a young man who aspired to be a chef. I simply gave him the magazine during our next session and pointed out the article. It cost me nothing (you *are* allowed to take the magazines), but it sent a powerful and encouraging message to him.

What Needs to Happen?

All young people, but especially those in emotional or psychological distress need ongoing reassurance they are cared for and cared about. That assurance is a strong component of resilience and the ability to handle times when life can be rough and rigorous. Indeed, life *will be* rough and rigorous for a child or adolescent who doesn't feel cared about. (It's no coincidence that, when we are angry and upset with a youngster, these messages and demonstrations of caring come to a halt.)

Utilize these interventions and build on them. You'll see a difference in the child, perhaps one that will surprise you. If you'll look closely, you just might find an even bigger difference in yourself.

Into our ears and attitudes: Keep in mind that, as I understand it, Dr. Hew Len's direct contact with his patients was limited. His statements of "I care about you" ("I love you") primarily were directed at his *own* ears and his *own* attitudes. What could happen if we learned to make communication to our own ears and our own attitudes a lifelong habit?

The difference it makes: My educator friend in California, Dr. Marvin Marshall, sent me a piece of correspondence from a teacher he had received. Since Marv and I are "peas in a pod" in our philosophy of affirming and directing young people, he thought it interesting and worth sharing. I pass it on with his approval and encouragement:

> *I have one child right now (fourth grade) and every single teacher he has ever had tells me nothing but horror stories about him. He is a delightful young man who has some serious learning disabilities but, because I built a nice relationship with him in September, he has been nothing but a joy this year.*
>
> *I can honestly say I have not had one single behavior issue with him, and it's not because*

I'm a great teacher and the others weren't. But in watching them with their classes, I can say they don't seem to care much about actually connecting with their kids on any level except, "I'm up here as the boss, and you'd better do as I say!" I even had one teacher inform me she tells her kids, "I'm the queen and this is MY kingdom." Lovely.

Chapter Thirteen

More Putting it to Work: "I'm Sorry"

Saying "I'm sorry" and meaning it can be a cleansing experience, an action that reverses the direction a mistake is heading. It can do wonders for both the giver and the receiver.

Many issues in the experience of the adult are not the child's issues, nor are they the child's fault. It's not the child's fault the company is laying off workers and that Mom and Dad are worried sick about it. And it's not the child's fault that state and federal achievement requirements have a teacher wondering how she's going to make the count this time. Although our young people figure into the stresses we face, they create fewer of those stresses than we might imagine.

(As was mentioned earlier, our children are like thermometers: They don't create the "weather" that blows into their day-to-day world; they only reflect it.)

Why is it So Difficult?

It's very difficult for some folks to apologize to a child. I'm not sure why that is, but I do know this: The more psychologically fragile the adult, the more difficult it is for them to apologize. I believe this is because an apology requires honesty and vulnerability. These create the capacity to recognize and admit a mistake in attitude or action. Indeed, there are those folks who feel they long ago met their lifetime quota on mistakes. That would make an apology difficult for them.

An authentic apology should show up in the changed behavior of the one apologizing. Isn't that the whole point? There again, some folks are too fragile to change, just like the teacher who was going to *wait* for the 13-year-old boy to do all the changing.

A "stuck" mom: At one time I was the consulting psychologist for a therapeutic group home, an emergency shelter for girls, and several units of a residential treatment facility. (They shared the same property and staff.) A 12-year-old came into treatment. She and her younger sister had been adopted by a pastor and his wife. The older girl began making things very difficult for her adoptive parents, especially Mom. She insisted on taking care of her little sister, just as she had done before they were adopted.

Things grew difficult to the point the mother could not manage the older sister at all. The girl was placed into the church-affiliated treatment program. She had many problems; my evaluation gave evidence of that.

In order to help the girl work on her issues as well and as quickly as possible, the facility and I discussed with the mother how she could help the girl the most. All she needed to do was tell the youngster that her removal from the family and placement into residential treatment was because of *her* issues (Mom's), not the girl's, and that she was truly sorry for any pain it had caused her.

Mom noted the idea was both true and that it made sense. We all sat down in our conference room, as I announced to the girl that her mother had something important to share with her.

Mom opened her mouth to speak, then a strange look came over her face. She said ... *nothing*! The girl's adoptive mother could *not* tell her daughter the one thing they both desperately needed to hear. Mom absolutely could not do it.

It Starts Inside

Keep in mind that Dr. Hew Len's expressions of "I'm sorry" were toward his criminally insane patients. Since there was difficulty with face-to-face communication, his expressions were first and foremost spoken into the ear of his own heart. Fortunately, his heart was listening. If I were speaking as a parent or teacher and attempted to put on that mindset, the processes of "I'm sorry" might sound something like the following:

I'm sorry for viewing your behavior as a planned attack against me rather than a signal that you were anxious and afraid.

I'm sorry for seeing you as a burden in my life (or career).

I'm sorry for sometimes shoving what I want in front of what you need.

I'm sorry for being so impatient with you. I'm the adult; I should act like it.

I'm sorry for deliberately avoiding you. That wasn't right.

I'm sorry for those times when I embarrassed you on purpose in front of your friends.

I'm sorry for lashing out at you without thinking. I know my words hurt you deeply.

I'm sorry for those times when anger clouded my judgement and caused me to act more like a child than you.

Here's one that's a bit more involved:

Mary, one of life's greatest questions might go something like this: Why do we struggle so with those we'd die for? If I ever had an answer to that question, I have misplaced it somewhere. I've misplaced it, Mary, not in my mind, but in my actions, my actions toward you. I'm sorry; I'm deeply sorry.

Don't get me wrong, Mary. There are those times when your behavior upsets me. Sometimes it upsets me a lot. But that's never an excuse for me to act even worse. As I said, I am sorry. I can and I will do better.

If I expressed any of these "I'm sorry" statements to a youngster and meant them, wouldn't it affect my next interaction with that child or teen? If, for instance, I sincerely said, "I'm sorry for shoving what I want in front of what you need," shouldn't that statement be backed up with the realization that my behavior was not only selfish and wrong, but that I needed to *change* that behavior? And wouldn't the next step be to work on ways to actually accomplish the changes? I believe this was Dr. Hew Len's point precisely.

When the recipient of my apology is a child or adolescent, it would be helpful to create opportunities to apologize to the youngster directly, unless doing so would create more damage than good. The apology should be made in a way that it would be supportive of the nature, age, and maturity level of the youngster.

A heartfelt, "I'm sorry," is rarely expressed in error.

How it affects a youngster: The sad truth is that young people receive precious few apologies from the adults in their lives. (The *why* of this could make another book in itself.) When an adult expresses an appropriate and heartfelt apology, it can have an unbelievably positive impact on the child. Youngsters are sophisticated enough to know we're not perfect; they appreciate our recognition of that fact from time to time.

It is possible a youngster will have difficulty with an adult's apology, although it's the sort of difficulty that actually reflects back positively on the relationship. A quick story puts some light on this possibility.

It's no secret that my wife and I raised a son who spread his share of difficulty during his teens. Bobbie attended a ladies' retreat offered by several area churches. One of the topics at the retreat dealt with how, as mothers, they treat their children when they are especially frustrated, upset, and angry with them. When she returned home from the conference, Bobbie sat down with the boy and apologized for her inappropriate behavior and angry mishandling of an earlier incident.

He struggled with her apology:

> *Mom, please. You don't have to apologize. I*
> *messed up. It was MY fault.*

> *Maybe you're right; but how I handled it was*
> *MY fault. I was the adult in that situation; I*
> *should have acted like it. I can do better, and I*
> *will do better, son. Again, I'm sorry. I hope*
> *you will forgive me.*

Of course, he forgave her. Things dramatically improved between them. He and his mother are extremely close today.

Relationships have turning points, those moments in time that either add to or erode the bond between individuals. A simple, well-placed and timely, "I'm sorry," can create a life-changing turning point.

An apology that shows: The most relationship-focused component of an apology is the *intent* to change as a result of the apology and the effort to make that change show in improved attitudes and behaviors. This sounds like it ought to be an automatic process, but it's not. People too often apologize for their behavior, then keep on making the same mistakes. What does that say about their apologies?

My wife loves to quote her father (he's the guy who had that little heart-to-heart chat with that junior high school principal): "*Show* me; don't tell me." (Our children heard that a few thousand times during their growing-up years.) *Showing* gives the "I'm sorry" substance and credibility. It's the "feet" of an apology.

Showing is the only thing that can take an apology past the moment of its expression.

Forgive Me?

The book, *Zero Limits*, and the lecture by Dr. Vitale I attended, noted how Dr. Hew Len also requested forgiveness from each of the criminally insane patients he served. Like the preceding "I love you" and "I'm sorry," the "Please forgive me" comment was more indirect than direct. I'm absolutely certain, however, its expression showed in the way he regarded and treated all the patients in his care there in the ward.

Asking forgiveness for thoughts, attitudes, preconceptions, and negative beliefs in such a manner would constitute something I would call prayerful "heart-talk." I can't think of a situation or circumstance where it wouldn't be appropriate, especially if the thoughts I worked on were mine.

A need for caution: It might not always be best to ask a child for forgiveness directly. Three reasons come to mind:

1. *By their very nature children are forgiving beings, anyway.* They haven't had the years to build up bitterness and resentment, so the notion of forgiveness is intact and natural.

2. *Forgiveness can be a confusing notion to a youngster, especially a really young child.* A request for forgiveness could make them uncomfortable, even anxious. It could cause them to revisit pain that might best be left unvisited. An appeal for forgiveness should build up, never tear down.

3. An active request for forgiveness expects a response. Pressure to respond to a forgiveness request could make a youngster uncomfortable. The whole point is to restore the relationship, not create another barrier. It we were truly sorry, why should the child have to take any action at all? In my wife's conversation with our son she said: " I hope you will forgive me," not "Will you forgive me?" That left the rest up to him.

I'm not suggesting here that I would always be hesitant to ask a young person for forgiveness. There will be those times when it would be the right thing to do. Leaving a youngster a note could be an excellent way to request forgiveness and not put the child under any immediate pressure. In all these instances, my focus would be the needs of the child or teen, not mine.

The Last Part: "Thank You"

The last part of the "cleaning" process Dr. Vitale covers in *Zero Limits* (as shared with him by Dr. Hew Len) is an expression of gratitude to the person being addressed. In its simplest context, it is a "Thank you" delivered in the same manner as the other parts of the "cleaning," whether it's done face-to-face or is delivered nonverbally to the person's essence and spirit.

I have spoken and written for years on the power of gratitude. Being thankful and appreciative redirects the focus away from one's self. Adults and children alike can simmer and stew in their own selfishness long enough to become blind to the cares and concerns of others. Words and gestures of "Thank you" change that focus and put it on others. It's not only a shift that's refreshing, it can be life-changing, perhaps even life-saving. Gratitude helps the giver every bit as much as the receiver. Here's an example:

Mary, I acknowledge the fact you are under no obligation at all to forgive my shortcomings, expressed or not. I am grateful when you do, as it helps me become a better parent (or teacher). Thank you.

You will notice that some of the sample dialogs of problem-solving in this book end with a statement of gratitude to the youngster. I see it as being as important as any other part of the process, and of the relationship.

What Needs to Happen?

Are the adults *always* focused on what's best for the youngster? Hardly. In our frustration and anger, we can focus on what *we* want until the "I'm sorry" never leaves its box.

A big obstacle: One of the biggest obstacles we must remove is the one to which many adults cling. They convince themselves their position as a parent or teacher justifies *any* behavior on their part. Whatever they do is by order of their authority. As absurd as it sounds, the belief that being a parent or teacher justifies all actions and behaviors has created untold barriers in relationships. And it has done some serious damage.

"I'm sorry" and "Thank you" are not weaknesses, they are strengths that get stronger and more effective with practice. They are right-setting strengths.

A reaffirming story: Let me close this chapter with a true account that reaffirms two powerful concepts: 1) Any change can happen quickly and, 2) when we make changes for the better, amazing things happen around us and *in* us. (This story comes from the seventh chapter of my book, *If My Kid's So Nice, Why's He Driving ME Crazy?* [Sutton, 1997]).

A mother I knew through my work in the public schools once approached me with a problem. Tearfully she told me her youngest son was failing ("D"s) two classes in school, although there was no logical cause or reason why he should be failing. The boy was bright, capable, and popular with his classmates, and he was a starter on the basketball team. (This was just before the implementation of "No Pass; No Play" in Texas.)

I sat down with her and outlined a strategy she and her husband might use with the boy, a strategy that would hopefully pull the problem out where they could work on it. She shared she would coach her husband on the strategy and use it with their son that very evening.

She was all smiles the next morning. "It worked!" she exclaimed. She went on to share how they both sat down with the boy after supper and how her husband opened the conversation.

Son, the fact that you're failing two subjects in school is unacceptable. It's also a puzzle to your mother and me. It doesn't make sense, given your ability. You should be passing easily. Is it that you don't understand the work or can't do it? Do we need to look for a tutor to help you?

150

The boy assured his parents he was capable of doing better, much better, than he was.

Then that takes us to another possibility, son. Perhaps there's something that's bothering you so much it's affecting your school work. If so, we'd like to know what it is so we can help you fix that problem, if we can.

He paused a moment, then went into the next part of the strategy.

It is possible that the problem has to do with your mother or me, or both of us. Perhaps it's something we have done or have said, or didn't do, or didn't say, that has affected you so.

He paused again and smiled at his son.

Being a parent is tough work sometimes. I know we ... I, have made mistakes along the way. If there's a problem or an issue with us, together or individually, please *tell us what it is so we can work on it right away. You know we love you and that we would never intend you harm deliberately.*

Now, you might be concerned about telling us what the problem is for fear we would become angry or upset, or because you'd be concerned about hurting our feelings. Please, we WANT to know. We won't love you any less, regardless of what you have to say. So, what's the problem, son? What is dragging down your grades so at school?

"I'm not sure, Dad," the boy replied.

Fair enough. Take some time and think about it. Then I hope you'll have an answer for us. Remember, son, we WANT to know.

Later that evening the boy approached his parents, telling them he knew what the problem was. He teared up as he looked into his father's face, then he held up one hand with the thumb and forefinger almost touching.

Dad, I feel about this big when you raise your voice at me. It's been going on for a long, long time but, as I've gotten older, I can hardly stand it anymore. When you scream and holler at me, Dad, it just tears me apart on the inside.

There's an old saying that goes, "Be careful what you ask for; you just might get it!" Dad got it, right between the eyes.

Mom shared that, to her husband's credit, he owned up to the problem. He made no attempt to rationalize or explain away his behavior. He apologized to the boy and promised to do better.

Dad *did* do better; a lot better. Mom shared the subject never again was discussed after that.

And the original problem, the boy's grades? They started coming up immediately. He never failed a class after that, and he had a strong standing in his graduating class.

Too perfect? Some might say this whole scenario had so much going for it that it was *too* perfect and *too* good in how it played out. I'll let others judge that. But considering the efforts we take with our own children, grandchildren, and students, shouldn't we work toward the best possible outcomes?

Part Three

Strengthening Change

Dealing with Feeling

Soothing: A Necessary Thing

One Foot in Front of the Other

Spit in the Soup

Fixing the "Where"

Fixing the "When"

Overhauling the Outcomes

Don't Stir the Pot

Mastering Noncoercive Response

Resolving Conflicts with Your Children

Exercising Acceptance and Forgiveness

Keep Asking "What Happens Next?"

Chapter Fourteen

Dealing with Feeling

As you can see, the remainder of this book addresses the empowering and strengthening of the sort of change in behavior that allows a youngster to be more that just functional. We're talking about total empowerment, empowerment to manage life as life brings the terms, whatever they are.

Sometimes those terms are painful; the child must hurt and suffer through them. It's a natural and normal process.

Suffering (we'll later consider the notion of "legitimate" suffering) is never optional. Folks who attempt to shortcut suffering pay a dear price for the denial they maintain and the emotional detours they take. Although children and adolescents are generally more healthy than adults in the way they manage change brought on by loss, they're always taking notes on the examples set by the adults closest to them. Sometimes that's good; sometimes it's not.

Good Grief

In my opinion, all shortcuts to suffering take the traveler on a winding side trip that makes the journey unbearably long and even more difficult over time.

A model for suffering: Anne Morrow Lindbergh showed us how to suffer well. Although she lived much of her life in the shadow of her husband, Charles A. Lindbergh, she was an exceptional human being. Yes, his life was rich with one accomplishment after another in aviation, science and medicine, literature, politics, and ecology. For the most part, Anne was at his side in these endeavors, plus she was an accomplished and award-winning author with 13 books to her credit.

Anne Lindbergh left her husband in the dust in one area: She had the ability to suffer well and with healing-bound purpose. The kidnapping and death of their firstborn (a son, Charles Jr.) in 1932 had to be the lowest point in her life. What event could possibly be more horrible? But she handled that loss and the media circus trial that followed "The Crime of the Century" with grace to spare. Years later, here's how she explained the experience of deep loss and suffering. It's from her book, *Hour of Gold, Hour of Lead*, (Lindbergh, 1973).

> *In the end, one has to discard shields and remain open and vulnerable. Otherwise, scar tissue will seal off the wound and no growth will follow. To grow, to be reborn, one must remain open and vulnerable—open to love, but also hideously open to the possibility of more suffering.*

It would be inaccurate to suggest that, following the death of his only child (there were other children later), Charles Lindbergh closed himself to the world. He didn't. Oh, he continually ducked the media (sometimes wearing disguises while traveling in public) and avoided reporters he did not trust, but he accomplished much in a wide range of endeavors. But Charles Lindbergh spoke little of the loss of his son and seemed to cover his pain with his work. I would say he did not suffer that loss well, and it might have cost him. History shows Anne survived Charles by more than twenty-six years. Was that a coincidence, or did Anne Lindbergh's ability to suffer a tragic loss and move through it make a difference in the quality and the quantity of her life?

Sometimes we can be so strong it hurts us.

In their own time: It would be ridiculous to "prescribe" a course of suffering. The how, when, where, and how long of suffering are unique to the personality and resources of each individual.

I believe suffering is much like crying in terms of achieving closure and returning to a pre-suffering state. How long should a person cry when they are overwhelmed emotionally? Answer: As long as it takes.

When should one *stop* crying? Answer: When they're done with it. Authentic tears are spontaneous; so is quality suffering. Anything else would be a performance, not the work of healing.

Sometimes the spontaneity of ours or others' tears and suffering catches us off guard. I once had a young patient whose mother was dying with cancer. The girl was living in a group home when the news came of Mom's death.

Her houseparents were concerned the news of her mother's death seemed to have little effect on the girl. I had two sessions with her and drew the same conclusion. During our third session, however, she ran toward me with a different expression on her face. She threw her arms around my neck (I was seated) and began sobbing uncontrollably.

"My mommy's dead!" she cried over and over again. She had absorbed the truth and its impact, and she did it on *her* schedule.

How do we know? How do we know when a youngster is experiencing difficulty in grieving? How can we know they are having difficulty processing emotionally powerful events and circumstances? How do we know when they are *not* suffering in a way that takes them steadily through the pain? Here are three markers that tend to be amazingly reliable.

1. *Changes in school performance.* Difficulty with concentration at school and falling grades can be indicative of trouble with the processing of loss. (In this case, loss could be just about anything that abruptly alters the structure in a young person's life.) The youngster simply can't focus on school tasks. This is especially the situation when a decline or drop in school performance falls within the same time frames as the events and circumstances of the loss. (It doesn't take a lot to figure this out, but it's amazing how often it's overlooked.)

2. *Changes in mood and relationships.* When normally agreeable and interactive youngsters become sullen, angry, and overly defensive, it should send up a red flag.

I experienced an episode of this in my own family. My mother struggled with cancer for more than two and a half years. It was difficult on everyone. As her condition worsened, I could read the impact it had on my children, especially the youngest one, my daughter. One day while I was holding IEP meetings at the elementary campus, her second-grade teacher approached me with a concern.

Jim, there's been a change in Katie. She's normally bright, bubbly, and in the center of everything. Now she seems easily upset and aggravated. She's overly defensive and, in my opinion, brisk, short, and "ugly" to anyone who says anything to her at all, including ME. Lately, she's starting to isolate, and that's just not like her. Any ideas?

I explained to her what I thought it could be, and asked that she send Katie to the library so I could speak with her. When she arrived, I took her to a small, side room and shared what I had heard.

Katie, I just spoke with your teacher. She told me your behavior at school has changed a lot ...

Before I could continue, she interrupted me mid-stream.

That's because she doesn't like me!

Honey, are you worried about Grandma?

The dam broke. Tears that child had been holding back for weeks and months gushed out all at once. She cried so hard her body was heaving back and forth. I held her tightly as we both cried that morning.

3. *Changes in eating and sleeping.* These can be early signs of a youngster's movement through grief. Although some difficulty with eating and sleeping is to be expected, abrupt and excessive change affects one's ability to function. Kids who struggle with grief sometimes stop eating, or they eat everything in sight. It's a good idea to check their body weight and monitor their meals during these times.

Sleep issues are common, but they can be a concern, as in the case of prolonged difficulty falling asleep or invasive, disturbing dreams or nightmares. Another clue might be the child who repeatedly falls asleep in class.

I had one patient, a ten-year-old girl, whose father was dying with cancer. She knew this; it was my job to help her process it. She told me one day that she had such trouble falling asleep that she'd sometimes take her cat into the living room. She would sit there and cry, holding her cat, sometimes for hours. (Obviously, her lack of sleep didn't fare well for her at school.)

When I shared this information with her parents, they had no idea it was happening. They agreed to check on her at night. If the girl was up, one of them would sit with her.

(Her father did an amazing thing for his daughter before he died. He wrote letters to her, letters to be opened at special times and events in her life: high school graduation, college graduation, first job, marriage, first child, and first grandchild.)

If a youngster is having nightmares, it's good to check for a recurrent theme. This can be a sign a youngster is "stuck" in the grief or is struggling to work through it.

I worked with one young lady whose brother was killed violently in a traffic accident as he was riding with another brother on a scooter. She shared the dream she had been experiencing:

My dead brother is on the kitchen table. He looks awful. His blood is covering the table. It's dripping over the sides. I'm crying, trying to catch my brother's blood in a bottle before it drips onto the floor.

She told me she had been having that same dream over and over again. I did some closure activities with her and, over time, the nightmare stopped.

A Feelings Primer

Suffering is best understood as a component of loss, but loss, experienced as sadness or depression, is only one emotional experience. Even then, it rarely gets stuck in the "On" position. It comes and goes. More importantly, sadness and suffering can be resolved. Young people need to know this.

Feelings can be overwhelming. Keeping concepts simple is critical to a youngster's understanding of what's happening to them emotionally and how they can manage it. When it comes to emotional "material" and understanding it, simplicity is the key.

I went to some training once and received a handout from the instructor. It was a page full of dime-sized feelings faces. There must have been 100 of them on that sheet. (I'm sure there weren't 100 on the page, but it certainly seemed like it.)

Too many! Unless one is attempting to evaluate a child's cognitive horsepower and the ability to discern the thin difference between "vengeful" and "outraged," why would we want to further confuse an already confused and hurting child? Where's the sense in that?

By keeping it simple, I'm suggesting we go from 100 feelings to four for starters. That's right, just four feelings, and not all of them are negative. I share these four feelings in the context of emotional growth and healing using this incredibly simple model. I call it "The Upside-down 'T' of Feelings." (The youngest person I used this model with was three years old; she got it immediately. The oldest person was almost 60. He didn't get it, and died self-medicating with heroin.)

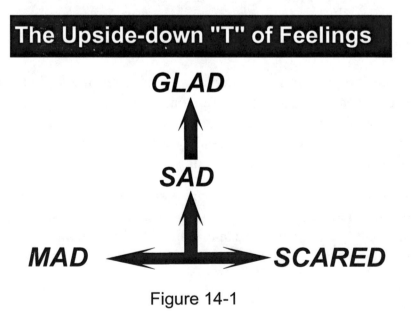

Figure 14-1

GLAD: Everyone wants to be happy and content, unless pain is their idea of a good time (and there are a few of those folks around). Unfortunately, the everyday impact of human experience dictates we won't stay in a glad, happy, or serene state *all* the time. (What does that say about people who smile all the time?) But it's a great place to visit and spend some time as often as we can.

GLAD is not necessarily an overt feeling of joy. It can be an experience of balance, serenity, and emotional equilibrium.

SAD (a benchmark): SAD helps *all* the feelings function. It processes the experiences of loss and brings the person through those experiences. There is no way to authentic serenity (GLAD) in difficult times without navigating the uncomfortable, but authentic and healing, experience of sadness.

(Speaking to sadness, Benjamin Franklin wrote, "When nature gave us tears, she gave us leave to weep." The occasion for this wisdom was the death of his four-year-old son to smallpox.)

There are two very inappropriate responses to sadness: One is the avoidance of sadness altogether; the other is an attempt to reach GLAD synthetically.

Avoidance of sadness: A lot of folks avoid even slight experiences of sadness. They never want to look at it or talk about it. They just hope it will just go away. But it doesn't go away. Ignoring sadness is like ignoring an infection: Accumulated neglect can bring serious illness, even death.

With some children and teens the message of avoidance is expressed as temporary: "I don't want to talk about that right now," or "I don't want to talk about it today." Too often the deeper thought is, "I don't want to talk about it, *ever*!"

Some of my best insights into children and adolescents came from adults who were hospitalized for drug and alcohol addiction. They often related to the pain of childhood as the bedrock of their misery. They were in a hospital, hundreds of miles from home, work, and family. Many had lost their job and their marriage was gone or in tatters. They had destroyed the youthful innocence of their own children. Some were left with this decision: Get help, go to prison, or die.

Through treatment, these patients were provided an ideal time and place to offload some stinking and hurting emotional baggage, yet many of them simply could not do it. I would leave a two-hour group session completely exhausted, feeling as if I had done battle with the devil himself. (Some might even say that was precisely the case.)

Synthetic happiness: Unfortunately, the world is saturated with individuals who attempt to manufacture their happiness. Drug, alcohol, and sexual addictions are predicated on the notion that, if one can just indulge enough, the pain will go away as something more pleasant fills the emptiness. The brief relief is a poor substitute for healing and serenity, but, for many, it's all they know.

For a child, the self-indulged distraction might be a new toy, a video game, or candy, but the attempt to deflect thoughts away from suffering is *exactly* the same as with adults. It amounts to a whitewashing of pain, and that's all. The desire to deflect, avoid, or paste over even appropriate suffering is at the root of much of the poor emotional and physical health folks experience today.

Pascal's insight: At very least, what is the price of a life of unhappiness? Blaise Pascal (1623-1662), a mathematician and physicist in the 17th-century, offered this explanation:

*All of man's problems stem from his inability
to sit quietly with himself.*

It would be interesting to sit down with Pascal and ask him to clarify this statement. I interpret it to infer that, when folks are not comfortable in their own skin and with their own thoughts, they approach an unhealthy state that, without intervention, only gets worse.

Here's the bottom line: Sadness *does* hurt, but at least it's real. There's a good reason why the line going through SAD in the diagram (Figure 14-1) points up. It's the authentic track to happiness and healing.

MAD: This feeling obviously represents anger, a valid and necessary emotion. I've heard anger described as the energy required to take action to resolve it.

Isn't that true? In an inappropriate sense, anger can cause a person to be terribly destructive. But it can also be turned into a positive direction and become the energy to do something constructive, to address the issue or problem. Positive or negative, anger is *always* a call to action. *Which* action then becomes the issue.

I believe we can systematically and educationally "sell" youngsters on a better plan for managing their anger, a plan that will minimize grief and consequences while it maximizes healing. If we can pull that off, a child or adolescent could work past the "here and now" disruption, discomfort, and pain. We could even spare them (and ourselves) hours of uncomfortable intervention and negative consequences. In essence, we would be teaching a life skill.

What would be the value of a life skill like that over the next 50-90 years?

It sounds easy enough, doesn't it? It's not. There's one incredibly simple reason why children and adults often choose to stay angry, and this reason lies at the core of all counseling and psychotherapy: *It's often more comfortable to remain angry than to look at the pain beneath it.* Put another way, anger for these folks is just too hot to handle.

This all serves to explain why the line ANGER sits on in the diagram runs sideways, not upward. Meaning: Folks who choose to remain angry will avoid some suffering alright, but they will also avoid opportunity for serenity and authentic healing and happiness in their lives. In short, they might function, but that's about all. What they miss could fill out a good life.

SCARED: Fear is a valid and necessary emotion. It is survival-based. As a guide to wisdom, fear keeps us from making friends with rattlesnakes or attempting to jump the Grand Canyon on a tricycle. With most people, fear effectively puts the brakes on impulsive decisions and plants the notion that staying alive (or staying employed) is better than a few moments of reckless glory.

Can folks deny they are afraid? Of course. Does that mean they have dealt with the fear effectively? Probably not. I can flap my arms and cluck loudly, but it doesn't make me a chicken.

Denial of fear can serve a short-term purpose, but it fails in the long haul. Fear might not be acknowledged, but it shows up in avoidance and poor behavior. It shows up in the unwillingness to take appropriate risks, or the taking of outrageous risks in order to show just how afraid they are *not.*

Long-term denial of fear can make folks sick. As much as they work at convincing themselves they are not afraid, the body knows better. The body deals only in cold, hard truth.

Like MAD, the emotion of SCARED goes horizontal, also. When emotional growth stops, we say a person "goes sideways." They shut down to only two emotions: anger and fear. That's it, anger and fear. Wouldn't that be a miserable way to live? No matter if they're eight or eighty, these folks are *not* happy campers. They are *not* the kind of people you'd want to spend much time with.

LONELY (a bonus): LONELY could be added as a fifth feeling, although the model works fine without it. (We have added it to most of the activities that follow, but it easily can be removed.) We are social beings, so affiliation and interaction with others is important. Below is a graphic showing where LONELY would be placed. (Loosely interpreted, we're including it here as a combination of SAD and SCARED.)

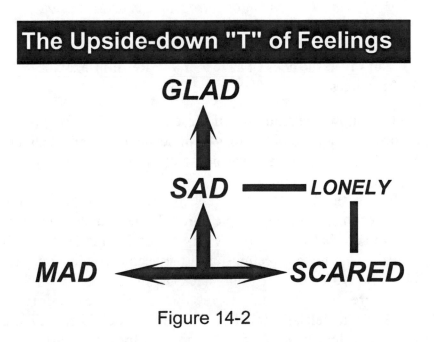

Figure 14-2

What Needs to Happen?

When youngsters understand their needs and feelings well enough to express an emotional state through them, they benefit in three powerful ways.

> 1. *They can communicate their concerns to caregivers more effectively.* In turn, it's more likely these concerns will be addressed. Result: Behavior improves.

> 2. *They communicate their concerns more effectively to themselves.* This is no small accomplishment, as it assists youngsters in understanding and addressing issues effectively on their own. Result: Behavior improves.

> 3. *Appropriate communication and expression can reduce the behavior-type expressions that had caused trouble and turmoil.* Simply put, if a child can *say* it, she doesn't have to *act* it. Result: Behavior improves.

What follows are a number of ideas and strategies for directly assisting a troubled child or teen in understanding and managing what is happening to them psychologically and emotionally.

Teach the feelings: We need to teach the model of the simple feelings to young people and help them understand it is accurate and that it applies to every living human being. Drill youngsters on the four feelings until they can correctly sort brief feelings scenarios on cards into stacks of the four (or five) feelings. Share examples and stories that check and reinforce a youngster's understanding of the model. Included here (Figure 14-3) are feelings "faces" that can be used for these activities.

Figure 14-3

Practice the feelings: Provide opportunities for youngsters to see, understand, and practice the feelings. Here are several activities that accomplish this well. Most of these and more can be found in *101 Ways to Make Your Classroom Special* (Sutton, 1999). They are included here with the permission of the author and publisher.

Ink or Oil? This exercise shows how it is possible for people to control, to a degree, how much they decide to let frustrating circumstances affect them. Since it is a visual exercise, it "connects" well with youngsters that have difficulty processing language.

Set up two large, clear glasses of water. Put a drop of ink into one of the glasses. Note how the ink is dispersed completely throughout the water, symbolizing how a bit of trouble affects some individuals. In other words, it "colors" *everything* about them from head to toe. The trouble goes completely through them.

Next, put a drop of oil into the other glass of water. Observe how it floats as a contained drop on the surface of the water. The rest of the water is unaffected by the drop of oil. The problem, that drop of oil, is still in the glass, but its dam- age is slight. It can be the same with people who encounter diffi-culty in their lives. The damage of the difficulty is minimal.

Discuss with the youngster or the group what it means for a person to accept difficulty as a drop of oil instead of a drop of ink. Also discuss how they might accomplish that difference.

A "spin" on this idea would be to show the activity to a couple of youngsters. Have them practice it until they can show it (and explain it) to others. Let them share the Ink or Oil? lesson to groups of three peers at a time. The groups then get together and write a collaborative explanation of the activity, what it means, and how it can be applied to situations in a person's life.

What was Lost? Here's an activity designed to help youngsters get more in touch with the concept of SAD as it per-tains to loss.

Assign youngsters to groups of three to five each. Provide them with this story or, better yet, read it to the whole group, being certain to make Johnny's age fit the age of the group. Encourage the group to identify all the things Johnny might lose.

Johnny is nine years old. He is very sad. His folks are getting a divorce. Johnny and his mother will move to another city when school is out. They will be living with Johnny's grandparents. Since depression is about loss, see how many things you can think of that Johnny will lose when he moves.

This activity brings up the distinction between tangible, intangible, and relationship losses. If possible, let the youngsters come up with these on their own, noting how not all losses are things you can touch and feel. Here are a few ideas to get started.

Tangible losses: His old home, his room, his desk at school, his basketball goal, his school, his church

Intangible losses: Security and order, confidence, the "way it used to be," an earlier standard of living

Relationships: His lifelong friends, his teachers, his school counselor, his school principal, his soccer team and coach, his father as a daily figure in his life

Pot Luck: Pot Luck means to go with whatever is provided. In this activity, youngsters elaborate on a feeling given to them by their birthday.

Each youngster, according to a feeling associated with the month of their birth (List A), writes a story about an object associated with their date of birth (List B). For instance, a youngster born on April 12th would write or tell the story, "I am a SCARED balloon." (Make it clear the story *must* begin with "I am a _____ _____".) Have them share their stories.

List A:	
January: SAD	July: GLAD
February: MAD	August: SCARED
March: GLAD	September: SAD
April: SCARED	October: MAD
May: SAD	November: GLAD
June: MAD	December: SCARED

Figure 14-4

171

List B:

1. flag	11. alarm clock	21. fish
2. cowboy boots	12. balloon	22. Sunday
3. baseball	13. turkey	23. school books
4. tricycle	14. ice cream cone	24. TV dinner
5. puppy	15. roller skates	25. uniform
6. calendar	16. sunflower	26. lawnmower
7. car keys	17. Christmas lights	27. ballpoint pen
8. sports car	18. kitten	28. truck
9. chick	19. necktie	29. birdhouse
10. earring	20. checkbook	30. tree
		31. watch

Figure 14-5

Here's a sample story, "I am a <u>MAD</u> <u>Sunflower</u>" (June 16th)

You know, sometimes it seems like even a sunflower can't get a decent break. You see, I love the sun. I love to admire it all day long. But there's this bunch of bees that keep walking on my face  and stepping in my eyes. It's like they have no consideration for a hard-working plant. I get so mad sometimes that I feel like going over to their hive and dropping a few petals in their way. Maybe then they'd get the idea that what they do really upsets me.

172

Hearts Apart: This exercise focuses on one of the most difficult things to teach: *empathy*. Thanks go to Stephanie Waters, a school counselor in Laplace, Louisiana, for this great idea.

Give each youngster in the class or group a large, construction paper heart. Ask them to write their name on their heart and pass it on to another student. (Use the same instruction for all, such as, "Pass it to the person behind you.") Explain this is an exercise in empathy, then discuss with them what empathy means. Share how this exercise demonstrates how they view certain circumstances as they would affect the person whose heart they are holding. Reinforce the notion that this is an exercise in assessing *another* person's feelings, not their own.

Provide the following list, or one similar to it, to each youngster, or project it on a screen. Ask them to tear off a piece of the heart they are holding as they feel each circumstance would affect *that* person. Have them write the letter on each piece as they tear it off, so the heart's owner can later see how a classmate empathized for them.

A. Tommy's dog is at the vet's. She was hit by a car.

B. Sarah just got word that Grandpa is back in the hospital.

C. Mark studied hard for the math test, but failed it.

D. Becky just found out her parents are getting a divorce.

E. Bobby ran his bicycle into a curb and broke the front wheel.

Finish the activity by having the youngsters tape the hearts back together and pass them back to their owners. Discuss the activity with them, focusing on how some situations are sadder than others, and how not everyone agrees when it comes to measuring what makes another person sad. Discuss also how difficult it is to "guess" at another person's feelings.

This Spud's for You! Give each youngster a potato and have them count off one through four (or five, if LONELY is used). The number they call corresponds to a feeling. (For example, #3 would be GLAD).

Students are asked to study their potato carefully, noting every feature of that potato that makes it different from every other potato in the world. They are to give their potato an identity, including boy or girl, name, and age. They are then asked to develop a story about their potato person, using the feeling assigned to them. Each youngster then tells the story about his or her potato person. As each story is finished, the potato goes back into the box.

*Look 'em over carefully, Miss.
They ALL look the same to me..*

At the end of the stories, when all the potatoes are back in the box, youngsters are asked to find their potato as quickly as possible. Later, ask them to explain just how they were able to pick out their potato from all the others. This makes an excellent lesson in understanding how everyone has features and qualities that make them unique and truly one-of-a-kind.

The Disk is Full! Here's an exercise that shows the effects of trouble in a person's life as it accumulates, and how we might help them. The inspiration for this activity came from Glenna Salsbury of Paradise Valley, California. (Glenna is an awesome speaker and past-president of the National Speakers Association.)

Show the youngster or the group a blank compact disk, a CD.

How many of you know what this is? That's right, it's a CD, a compact disk.

If it's blank, how much do you think it is worth? A few cents, maybe? It's almost worthless, isn't it?

Underscore the point by dropping the disk on the floor, then step on it "accidently" as you walk across the room. Point back to the disk on the floor.

It weighs less than an ounce, not much at all. But what if I were to store something very valuable on that CD? What if it contained something like the cure for all cancer. What would it be worth then? More, I'll bet; a LOT more!

If it were that valuable, I'd take better care of it, wouldn't I? I would treat it differently.

Pick up the disk, dust it off and, using both hands, gently place it on the desk.

If it is a full disk containing the cure for all cancer, what does it weigh now? Actually, it weighs the same as when it was empty. That's because the knowledge on the disk doesn't weigh anything. Knowledge is so important, yet you can't touch it or hold it in your hand. We can only touch and hold the disk the knowledge is on.

It's the same with us. Our brain is like a big CD, but the brain can't live without the body that carries it and takes care of it. And, like the CD, the brain can store lots of knowledge that we use to live better and help others live better, also.

Can we help others fill their CD, to gain learning and knowledge?

Hopefully, you'll get some agreement.

It's possible, isn't it, that mean people can try to destroy or hurt someone's CD? How might they try to do this? By telling them they are stupid or that they have no value? That could hurt a person's CD, couldn't it?

176

Would a person who has part or all of their CD hurt or damaged have trouble? What kind of trouble?

The discussion here might include how the person might lose their confidence or feel bad about themselves. They also might have trouble learning, and they might be scared most of the time.

How could we help them?

The discussion here could go in a lot of directions, but it generally amounts to the building up, not the tearing down, of others.

Too Hot to Handle! This activity comes from the book, *60 Ways to Reach a Difficult and Defiant Child* (Sutton, 2007). Anger is a good thing. It acknowledges an attack on one's self. Anger moves one to immediate action, which is why it easily can be turned in the wrong direction.

But staying angry is also a problem, especially if it continues on and on. As anger helps to cover our more vulnerable feelings (like embarrassment, failure, and humiliation), it hurts less to *remain* angry. So a lot of folks, children *and* adults, decide to stay angry as a way of being insulated from further pain. They protect themselves, but they also drop out of life in ways that matter greatly.

Here's a story that explains how anger works and why it is not intended to be a feeling that is permanently stuck in the "On" position. (If I were working with a boy, the name might be Sam, not Susan.)

Susan goes to the stove to take a pot off the burner. But when she touches the handle of the pot, it burns her. Her hand hurts. It hurts a lot! Susan finds a big oven mitt in the kitchen. It's perfect. She puts the big oven mitt on her hand so she doesn't get burned again.

Susan doesn't get burned again, so she keeps the mitt on her hand. Even when her mother tells Susan to move all the pots and pans from the pantry to the bottom drawer in the kitchen cabinet, she keeps the mitt on her hand.

Those pots aren't even hot, but no matter. She keeps the mitt on. Susan doesn't want to *ever* get burned again. She keeps the mitt on when she sweeps the floor, when she does her homework, and when she goes to bed. She even wears the mitt to school the next day. Susan doesn't want to get burned again.

Susan meets a new student at school and shakes her hand ... with an oven mitt on her own hand. The new student thinks Susan is a little strange. Her friends try to get her to take off the mitt.

But Susan's scared. She might get burned again. What should she do?

This is such an obvious scenario, you should get plenty of responses to it. Then, of course, you draw the example back to anger and how it can be used to protect us from emotionally being "burned" again. The aim would be to remove the mitt (anger) when its purpose has been served. It's a decision to deal again with life's situations bare-handed.

This would be a good place to share again Anne Lindbergh's comment on managing hurt and sadness. (It's on the second page of this chapter.)

Warn about denial and minimization: Denial and minimization strive to rub out reality. (Much like a feelings eraser.) This person would say that something did not happen at all or that it's not the big deal folks are making it out to be. Either way, denial and minimization shut down feelings, causing a person to be stuck somewhere short of the healing they need.

Part of the problem in addressing denial and minimization with young people is their small collection of experiences. They simply haven't been on the planet long enough to fully grasp that, over time, the impact of even the most difficult experiences fades. For them, denying the pain, or putting it into a smaller box, is a reasonable "fix." They have yet to learn how unresolved pain has a way of getting out of that box.

(I really must note here the importance of patience while working with young people on these issues. If they haven't learned what they *don't* know, forcing it on them might only aggravate already poor behavior. Unfortunately, there are many adults who remain as emotionally inexperienced as a young child. That topic could fill *another* book, couldn't it?)

Aren't you normal? Here's a "help-them-get-their-boat-off-the-rocks" strategy I have used many times with children and teens. It involves the use of paradox. On balance, it works very well to get discussion going in a more productive direction.

179

Let's say I'm concerned that Tommy isn't fully processing the loss of his grandmother. I start the dialog:

Tommy, you told me you and your grandmother were close, that you and she did lots of things together.

We did.

But her death didn't affect you much?

Not so much. She was very old. She was going to die sooner or later.

Tommy, I was 23 years old and in the service when I received word that my grandmother had died. It left a hole in me that lasted for some time. It would be normal for young folks like you to be sad and upset when someone that close to them passes away. Yet you told me it didn't bother you that much. Tommy, in every way I can think of, you look pretty normal to me. Can you tell me why you think you're NOT normal?

This dialog will either open the discussion or get you punched in the face.

Denial and minimization have a purpose: They buy time for one to absorb the impact of what has happened. (How often has someone responded to tragic news with, "Oh, no, that *couldn't* be." They're not accusing the news bearer of lying; it's simply a defense, a desperate hope there was a mistake.) Just like the young girl who on her own came to the realization her mother was dead, most children process loss in a way that works for them.

Buying some time: I read a study on a girl whose grandmother had died. Peers attempted to console her. They were shocked, however, when the girl said her grandmother's death was only a rumor, that the lady was in Europe on a buying trip for a chain of department stores.

Folks, Grandma was *dead*! Still, the girl's grades, overall mood, relationships, and sleeping and eating patterns didn't stumble. Her behavior was fine. In short order, she began speaking of the loss of her grandmother.

If a loss-affected youngster's performance and behavior are not at-risk, I see no need to shock them into my version of their reality.

Emphasize the value of legitimate suffering: It hurts to hurt, but it's the only authentic way to get to the top (GLAD). Here's a little graphic I developed years ago for use with children and adults. It's a great tool to use with individuals or groups. I believe it says a lot about suffering.

I often encourage counselors and therapists to make up a sign like this one. I suggest they put it on the wall with a chair beneath it. It makes three points about what we need to know about the healing aspects of true suffering.

Legitimate Suffering
permitted
HERE

30 minutes
free parking

1. *It should be legitimate and authentic.* It should not be contrived or designed to become a permanent tool for manipulating others. It's alright, even appropriate and expected, to ask for help and support from others who care. It's *not* alright to make them one's emotional hostages. Also, the graphic suggests the need and the course of suffering is unique to every individual.

2. *Some places are better places to suffer than others.* The "where" of suffering can make a difference in outcomes. Problems can erupt when one attempts to suffer in the *wrong* place.

3. *Suffering should never be open-ended.* Although suffering progresses on its own timetable, there comes a time for it to stop. The goal is for an individual to work *through* the suffering and eventually be done with it. One is not to become so bogged down that suffering starts to feel comfortable. Suffering is commendable; professional suffering is a disease.

Chapter Fifteen

Soothing: A Necessary Thing

The issue of self-soothing is a *huge* one, as many youngsters simply cannot soothe themselves in times of stress and difficulty. They rely on others to do it for them. As mentioned earlier, they seek continued soothing in food, toys, or activities of distraction. (Is it possible today's concern about childhood obesity could be connected to problems with self-soothing?)

These youngsters run the clear risk of carrying their self-soothing deficiencies into adulthood. There the stakes become even higher: broken and revolving-door relationships, bouts of unemployment, and overdependency on pills, alcohol, and "stuff" to ease their discomfort. They often leave in their wake children who can't learn from them what can't be taught.

Efforts spent on teaching youngsters skills of self-soothing can pay off today and into tomorrow. I believe we *must* make that effort.

Tough Shoes to Fill

Emotionally, adults differ from children in a number of ways. One critical difference is the capacity to draw upon one's own physical, psychological, and emotional resources to manage moments of trouble and difficulty. This capacity is developed over a lifetime of experiences, experiences younger folks do not yet have. (Most adults have this capacity, but some do not.) Simply put, it's the ability to self-soothe. It represents a powerful benchmark of maturity and resiliency.

If you'd like a strong glimpse of the value of self-soothing, put yourself in this person's shoes for a moment.

> He was shot out of the sky over North Vietnam in the winter of 1966, sustaining serious injuries. The enemy threw him into solitary confinement in a prison POWs called The Hanoi Hilton. In addition to being sick, cold, injured, and starving, he was tortured for information and a confession to war crimes. He remained a prisoner there, separated from health, home, and loved ones for seven years and nine days.

Try out your self-soothing skills on that scenario. This is from the real-life account of my friend, retired Navy Captain Jerry Coffee. You can read his whole story in his book, *Beyond Survival* (Coffee, 1990).

Jerry shares how he survived that experience on the strength of his spiritual faith and the relationships he had built all through his life. (His training as a Navy pilot was certainly a factor, also.) These experiential resources helped him affirm and reaffirm to himself that he was much more than the painful experiences of the moment. In fact, he's quick to credit high school literature teachers for insisting he memorize poems and prose. Classic poetry, as well as Bible verses he had memorized as a child, pulled him through some incredibly difficult times.

Although Jerry continues to be regarded a hero for the way he managed those experiences more than 45 years ago, he is quick to note he was not at all unique in that ability. (Perhaps humility is part of self-soothing, also.)

Young children don't have a deep well of experiences from which to draw their soothing. They often have no reference for knowing the problem of the moment is not a catastrophe, or even that they will survive it. Older children have a better perspective simply because they've experienced difficulty in the past and *know* the world didn't end there. Still, they sometimes struggle, also.

When a youngster cannot self-soothe, he goes into a "Someone, *please* soothe me!" mode as he turns to relationships, activities, and things to comfort him. His needs are desperate, and his behaviors too often reflect that desperation.

Not all young people are this desperate in their need for soothing, of course, but all can benefit from simple ideas and strategies that focus on becoming one's own best friend and resource in times of difficulty.

(Obviously, we strive to comfort and console our children when they hurt. Not to do so would be cold and indifferent. But when support is in short supply, as in Jerry Coffee's powerful story, we must learn to become our own best caregiver. Parents, teachers, and counselors should step in to model and teach this lifelong skill.)

Breathing on the Square

When individuals are under stress, their breathing is affected. They are physically and emotionally preparing to run or fight. They often are gasping and panting, not breathing. Consequently, much-needed oxygen doesn't get to the brain as it should, especially when panic begins to override reason. It's a rapid recipe for things getting worse in a hurry.

Here's an activity that was shared by a teacher in Tennessee. She used it with her students just before they were to take an important test. She instructed her class to do the following in four-second intervals:

    1. Breathe in slowly.

    2. Hold that breath.

    3. Breathe out slowly.

    4. Pause before starting over at the top.

The whole process, the square, takes 16 seconds. If a youngster does this correctly, the gasping and panting *have* to stop. Systematic breathing brings in oxygen and, more importantly, a sense of order and control.

It's not difficult to create a model of a square with four segments to each side as a visual guide (Figure 15-1).

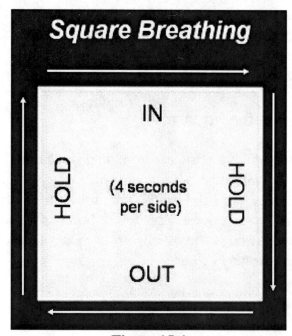

Figure 15-1

This graphic can be drawn on a piece of paper or it can be drawn on the floor. Another idea would be to use something like square stepping stones or small carpet samples and have the youngsters actually move through the square as they perform the breathing.

There is a powerful additional benefit: This breathing intervention provides a sense of focus. For 16 seconds the youngster's mind and focus are on completing the square, that's all. This reduces impulsive behavior, and it shows the youngster she *can* self-soothe. Simple, yet powerful.

If the child were to "breathe the square" a dozen times without stopping, she would have gone more than three minutes on the soothing she's provided for herself. More importantly, consider the possibilities of what all *didn't* happen while she was breathing the square.

The next step would be to encourage youngsters to do this on their own, to use Breathing on the Square as a resource they can call on to soothe themselves anytime, anywhere. Give it to them as an assignment, to try it and report back on later.

Okay, a youngster walking four-second turns in a mall or supermarket might look a tad conspicuous. Let them know it's just as easy to walk and breathe the square in a *straight* line as the seconds are counted off. The strategy and the benefits are the same.

More Soothing Activities

Here are a few more soothing activity ideas.

Bubbles! A bottle of plain soap bubbles can work some powerful magic in soothing. Simply ask the child to blow the largest bubble she can blow. A deep breath is her first response. (As mentioned, kids on the verge of panic don't breathe well.) Blowing a large bubble requires slow and sustained effort, as well as a point of focus. The benefits are realized quickly.

Patient popping: Once the youngster can blow a dozen or so large bubbles, add another element to the activity. Have the child stand about six to eight feet from you as you blow a large bubble toward her. Tell her she is to pop the bubble, but *only* when it reaches her. Impatience and impulsivity might cause her to shuffle her feet as the bubble approaches, but a little practice works miracles. The waiting on the bubble manages impulsivity and serves to restore control. The youngster learns she *can* wait.

Switch roles with the child to let her experience both the blowing and the popping of the bubbles. I would work toward removing myself from the activity and let two youngsters take turns with the activity. Create as much peer involvement as possible, as they will have access to peers for a lifetime.

(In my early use of bubbles as a therapeutic activity with young people, I never considered it would work with adolescents. I was pleased to discover I was wrong. Older kids enjoy the brief privilege of playfully regressing a bit, provided they are not embarrassed about it. With adolescents, younger-age activities might suit their level of emotional maturity perfectly. This comes with some sensitivity and vulnerability, so effort should be made to protect them from being seen by peers. With this understanding, simple, younger-child activities do surprisingly well with adolescents.)

Although using bubbles in this fashion demonstrates soothing, it isn't really self-soothing unless youngsters use them on their own to soothe and decompress. So encourage young people and their parents to add bubbles to their soothing supplies.

Control Cream: Here's another great idea for self-soothing; it's simple and effective. It was shared by a teacher in Idaho.

She purchased a cheap bottle of hand lotion, the kind with the little pump on top. She then went to the computer and created a special label for the bottle: Control Cream. She asked her students to let her know whenever they felt anxious. When a student alerted her as such, she would give them a couple of squirts of the lotion and tell them to slowly rub it into their hands.

She reported this strategy as being wonderfully effective. After awhile, she only needed to keep the bottle on the corner of her desk. Student would serve themselves as needed.

That's *self*-soothing, isn't it? It doesn't matter if you use lotion, cream, or oil, the end result is the same: tactile-kinesthetic soothing and a bit of time to manage the discomfort and impulsivity.

Control Balm: A high school teacher in Wyoming shared how he didn't think the idea of a bottle of lotion would go over very well with older students. We brainstormed that challenge and came up with an interesting alternative for at-risk adolescents.

The idea was to give the youngster a tube of lip balm with the instruction to use it whenever he felt especially anxious, vulnerable, or impulsive. The student he had in mind used the idea. The teacher later reported the Control Balm intervention was effective in providing necessary soothing as it bought some much-needed time.

Obviously, it's critical a youngster buy into the imagery of this intervention and let the balm help them soothe. (This can be quite a stretch for those youngsters who have been depending on others to soothe them.)

Brush-on soothing: A Special Education teacher who had once been an emergency room nurse shared a great idea for soothing a young, frightened child. She would take a soft-bristle brush and gently brush the youngster's forearms as she spoke to the child in a soothing, supportive voice.

This teacher often used this same intervention with students at school. She did note the importance of reading the child carefully, as some youngsters are overly sensitive to touch.

This would be an excellent activity for a parent to use with an especially tense and stressed young son or daughter.

The Peace Blanket: One teacher cut up an old souvenir blanket into smaller pieces. She would drape one of these pieces over the shoulders of an anxious or distressed student, noting to the youngster it was a Peace Blanket. She would inform the child how the blanket would help her regain control and composure.

The Privacy Desk: This simple and effective idea comes from Karen Ledet, a fourth-grade teacher at Vernon Elementary School in Vernon, Florida.

Unassigned desks or small work tables are placed along perimeter walls of the classroom to provide privacy and space (NOT punishment) for students who are having difficulty working next to others, or who are experiencing some distress or frustration.

These are not used for full-time seating. On occasion, I might recommend the move, but I prefer to leave it up to the students.

Angry and frustrated students especially seem to enjoy having a place to cool down with no issues or commotion. Low attention is given to this. The idea MUST be presented as a way to help youngsters successfully maintain control and composure.

Karen found an excellent way to not only help youngsters avoid a major meltdown, she encouraged them to monitor themselves, a skill they can use in *any* environment. It's also interesting to note Karen does not use a regular teacher's desk in her classroom; she uses a large table, instead. Half of the table is cleared for use as a Privacy Desk.

(It's interesting, isn't it, how some youngsters seem to need twice as much space around them as others? Equal columns and rows of desks in the classroom might be a recipe for trouble with those students needing more space around them. Karen's idea, the Privacy Desk, is sensitive to this issue.)

Parents: Although these suggested activities were shared by teachers, it should be a simple matter to adapt them to the home environment.

Make a Soothing "Appointment"

Good counselors know there's a thin line between being an emotional resource to a child and being a too-available crutch. (Therapists have precisely the same concerns with adult patients.) The solution for the "being too-available" problem is for the counselor to offer praise and encouragement to the youngster who does *not* come to them between scheduled visits. (This could be one drawback to a school counselor being physically close and available.)

When the child or teen is encouraged to gather their troubles and bring them to the regularly scheduled appointment, they are implementing more tolerance, a kind of self-soothing. Of course, it's important for the counselor to encourage the youngster to continue to use and expand this valuable skill.

Parents and caregivers can create much the same outcome. It's critical, however, that a specific and predetermined time, the "appointment," be established for sharing. If this isn't done, the whole process comes across sounding to the youngster like, "Just deal with it and don't bother me about it, *ever*!" Appointments should be kept.

Address the Physical Cues

Youngsters in deep emotional turmoil can't really put off being soothed. When they experience temporary difficulty they should learn to tolerate and manage, however, a focus on changing immediate physical cues can be helpful.

All emotional distress comes with physical cues, specific elements of fear and tension that work on the body. These can be changed with conscious and deliberate effort on the child's part. The better the capacity to change physical cues in times of stress, the better the ability to self-soothe.

The important thing about addressing physical cues is not what youngsters do to alter physical cues of fear and distress, but that they *do* something to modify their physical experience of the moment. It represents a small bit of empowerment, but it comes at a time when *any* empowerment is helpful. Although these simple actions might not change the circumstances that caused the distress, they do focus on something youngsters *can* control (see Figure 15-2).

Addressing the Physical Cues

A child who feels her body getting tense can focus specifically on making her body relax a bit.

A child who is not breathing well can focus on breathing, perhaps even use the Breathing on the Square activity.

A child who is tense and standing simply can sit down. A child who is tense and sitting can stand up.

A child who is tense and dry-mouthed might drink a glass of water slowly.

Figure 15-2

Remember the Reminders

It's a general practice of adults to evaluate present events and circumstances against past experiences. There's *always* a high-water mark for joy, sorrow, fear, and all emotional states. With a bit of reflection, most of us can recall our own high-water marks.

The chances are good that our high-water mark for an experience is *not* what's happening at any given moment. (If it is, then it's a *new* mark for evaluating future events and circumstances.) On balance, we've had higher highs and lower lows than we are currently experiencing and, more importantly, we *know* we have survived them.

The act of considering a current experience against an extreme mark for a similar event can be a soothing reflection for older children. They've been around just long enough to make a few deposits and withdrawals from their bank of experiences. Younger children have more difficulty making these comparisons because of fewer experiences. This is precisely why even minor events can disturb them so.

Reminders are a way to put a better frame on an uncomfortable experience. (The mental activity of putting a better frame on what has happened is called "reframing.") Here are some reminders, reframing statements a youngster can use as another way of self-soothing:

> *Hey, I KNOW I've handled stuff tougher than this before.*

> *This isn't really as bad as it looked at first.*

> *I can handle this because I've handled worse.*

> *I'm up to the challenge this time.*

> *You know, there's really no need for me to turn this into World War III.*

"Self" and Soothing

The capacity for a youngster to self-soothe is directly related to that child's concept of self. This is Self-Concept; the youngster's evaluation of it makes up Self-Esteem. When a youngster improves or gains in Self-Concept, his ability to self-soothe improves also. They move together. It makes sense then that efforts at improving Self-Concept could boost skills of self-soothing substantially.

In addition to Self-Esteem, there are three other components to Self-Concept: Body Self, Social Self and Cognitive Self. It's not at all unusual for a youngster to struggle with one or more of these. This is where we can help.

Body Self: Body Self relates to how a youngster views her physical appearance and presence in comparison to peers. Although we can't always change every aspect of how our children look, the best appearance or correction possible is important, whether it be clothing, braces, eyeglasses, or any number of things that enhance appearance and a sense of physical wholeness. In other instances, Body Self might be related to physical skills and abilities. Sports and athletics would be an example. Helping a youngster with these skills contributes powerfully to Body Self.

Social Self: Social Self reflects a youngster's level of comfort in being around and interacting with others. Like any other skill, it can be developed. Consider also how Social Self is critical to self-soothing. If a youngster is socially adept enough to ask others appropriately for help or assistance, they likely are getting all the soothing they need.

Cognitive Self: Cognitive Self is closely tied to self-soothing. It's the ability to use skills of thinking and accumulated knowledge to solve problems and issues. A child who is failing in school is experiencing a major problem with Cognitive Self. Helping a child with homework or finding a good tutor for them addresses Cognitive Self. The practice of commenting on a youngster's good decision-making ability addresses Cognitive Self, and it encourages the child to keep up the effort. A child with a stronger Cognitive Self finds it easier to self-soothe.

All four of these, Self-Esteem, Body Self, Social Self and Cognitive Self are interrelated. When we improve a youngster's capacity in one or more of them, the whole Self-Concept receives a boost. When that happens, improved skills of self-soothing follow.

What Needs to Happen?

Like so many issues addressed in this book, the need for soothing is hardly limited to children and teens. It's a need that travels with us through life. (My mother passed away in 1986, yet there are still those times when I surely could use her approval and reassurance.)

As a matter of fact, I'd be considerably concerned about *any* individual who claimed never to need soothing. Such a person would be unusual, indeed. They would seem to be oblivious to the forces and factors of life itself.

How do we know when a youngster understands a need for soothing and knows how to address it in a way that reflects empowerment and growth? The following three points come to mind:

> 1. *They will be tuned in to the need for soothing and reassurance.* This means they accurately can assess elements of emotional discomfort and distress. It also means they are intuitive enough not to linger in discomfort to the point of panic, if they can help it. If they need assistance, they seek it; if they must go it alone, they earnestly try to make the best of it.

> 2. *They are capable and motivated to self-soothe, when necessary.* My Navy pilot friend, Jerry Coffee, managed this well under some extreme circumstances. He certainly knew he would not have much help in solitary confinement.

Efforts at self-soothing require more than just a collection of skills and activities. One must actually view them as viable and logical options for *them*. A teen can learn the Control Balm strategy for self-soothing, but if he feels the idea is silly and senseless, he will not use it. (Or, if his need for soothing has grown to panic proportion, he might trash the Control Balm and latch onto another person for the soothing.)

3. *They know when the need for soothing has passed, and they act accordingly.* This one is critical. The need for soothing is like the need for water. If you don't get enough, you'll perish; if you get too much, you'll drown. Balance is the key.

A very critical part to teaching a child or teen to self-soothe is the skill of putting away an intervention when it is no longer needed. In its best form this is not an instruction to the youngster, but rather an internal message. It's the child, for instance, who removes the Peace Blanket from her shoulders and places it in the stack with the others. It's the student who eventually leaves the Privacy Desk and returns to his assigned seat.

Although it's best these "putting away" gestures be completely voluntary, a quick comment to the child in recognition of a gesture could be helpful. A youngster's awareness of reestablished emotional stability is a big deal. It represents a giant step forward.

Chapter Sixteen

One Foot in Front of the Other

Before my wife and I built our current home, we lived 28 years in a home near the schools. Our children grew up in that house; it holds a ton of memories.

We built a large gazebo-like deck out in the back yard of that place. It was strategically anchored between two enormous oak trees. (I wrote my books from that deck.) Stepping stones would take me from the back porch of the house to the steps of the deck.

I could walk those stepping stones with my eyes closed. I didn't have to see or think about where I was going, so long as I reached the next stone, then the next, until I arrived at the deck. It was automatic, just like in the old saying: "Just keep putting one foot in front of another and you'll get there."

I *always* got there.

Behavioral Stepping Stones

Imagine the activity of walking out to that deck as one of bad behavior. In this example, the bad behavior is reinforced and strengthened every time the next stepping stone is reached. Ultimately, the purpose of the behavior, the payoff (arriving at the deck), would be realized.

This little analogy shows us why poor and inappropriate behavior keeps right on happening over and over again. A youngster keeps following the old familiar steps to a strong and predictable

198

payoff. Meanwhile, the adults involved often find themselves following familiar steps of their own, steps leading to the same ineffective interventions. It's a good formula for frustration, but not much change. (We had a saying in drug and alcohol treatment: "If nothing changes, nothing changes.")

What's Happening Here?

The behavior has become patterned. It is self-reinforcing, so long as the same steps lead to the same payoff. Typically, there are four components to a pattern. All of these are necessary for a behavior to maintain. Conversely, if any of these components were to disappear, the behavior could not continue. (There aren't many guarantees in the behavioral sciences, but this is one of them.)

> 1. *The behavior itself.* In our analogy, this would be the walk to the deck.

> 2. *The location or "where" of the behavior.* This would be represented by the stepping stones that always lead to the same place, the outcome of the behavior. The strength of the payoff in the outcome (and there always *is* one if behaviors continue over time) reassures the validity and certainty of the path taken to get there. (In other words, if the stones keep taking you to the deck, it *is* the right path.)

> 3. *The time or "when" of the behavior.* Every behavior happens sometime; no behavior can exist outside boundaries of time. Going back to our analogy, would it matter if I made that trip out to the deck on a clear and sunny day or on a freezing, pitch-black night? Of course, it would.

4. *The payoff of the behavior.* In this example, the payoff would be the outcome of the walk, the arrival at the deck.

Scattered Stones

Our hypothetical walk to the deck provides us with the elements we need to change the behavior. (We're speaking here of tactical change: stopping the occurrence of the behavior. Good intervention would also include strategic measures for identifying and addressing causes behind behavior, as we considered in earlier chapters. Remember: Occurrence and cause are two sides of the same coin.) Consider these four:

1. *Interrupt or redirect the behavior.* If it were raining, or if the sprinklers were going full-blast, I probably would not go out to the deck at all. What if the telephone were to ring as I stepped toward the first stepping stone? Or what if my foot was sore or injured? What if I was sick? All of these could affect whether I walk out to the deck at all.

2. *Alter the "where" of the behavior.* If someone were to remove some of the stepping stones or scatter them around the yard, the walk to the deck would *not* be the same. I might still get there, but it wouldn't feel *right*. The change would make me uncomfortable. In fact, I might become so distracted and distraught over my stepping stones being messed up I'd never make it to the deck at all.

3. *Alter the "when" of the behavior.* What if someone had kept me so busy during the day that the *only* time I could go out to the deck and work on a manuscript would have been after midnight? One can't very well work in the dark; deck walk cancelled.

4. *Dismantle the payoff.* If someone were to tear down my deck, the walk would no longer matter. The stepping stones would have no significance.

What Needs to Happen?

Unfortunately, it's all too easy for patterns of bad behavior to develop and to flourish. More importantly, it's all too easy for us, the adults, to become locked tightly into the situation, emmeshed into the pattern. Instead of solving the behavior, it's very possible for us to become a big part of it.

Here's a suggestion. Go back over this chapter and replace the deck analogy with some real behaviors you see daily, especially those that have been resistant to change. Dissect them in terms of behavior, location, time, and payoff. See if you don't uncover some excellent points for intervention. My guess is you'll not only find them, you'll find the process is helpful in addressing *all* problem behaviors.

We will now dig deeper to address the elements of behavior, location, time, and payoff in the next four chapters.

Chapter Seventeen

Spit in the Soup!

Is this chapter title descriptive enough? Do you get a picture? Chances are, if you're having lunch with your best friend and you lean over and spit in their soup, there are a number of things you might say to punctuate your behavior. One thing you could *not* say is, "Oh, I'm sorry; *that* was an accident!"

Hey, there's just no way you could disguise spitting in someone's soup as an accident. It's a provocative behavior and, very likely, it would provoke *plenty*.

Provoking Changed Behavior

The "Spit in the Soup" approach to redirecting oppositional or defiant behavior is as provocative as the behavior. It provokes the child or teen to do something *other* than the intended behavior. Drawing on our analogy from the last chapter, this approach would stop the walk to the deck altogether (such as making the telephone ring or turning on the sprinklers). What follows are some "Spit in the Soup" scenarios.

Mom's note to Johnny: I mention a strategy called the Important Things to Remember Board in my book, *If My Kid's So Nice, Why's He Driving ME Crazy* (Sutton, 1997). It's a simple message board placed in a prime location where all family members can see it. Everyone, parents and children alike, can use the board to alert family members to important upcoming situations, appointments, and events.

202

The Important Things to Remember Board carries with it one hard and fast rule: *Everyone* is responsible for reading what's on the board daily. "I didn't see the note!" would *not* be an acceptable excuse.

Mom hands Johnny the following note one morning, asking him to post it on the board.

Dear Johnny:

At 7:00pm this evening we are going over to the Smiths' house for dinner. The last time we went over there, you were twenty minutes late getting home, and we had to wait on you. It was not a pleasant evening for any of us.

I was just wondering ... should I worry about you being late again? Please check one below, and leave this note on the table.

_____ No problem, Mom. I will be ready to go at 7:00pm.

_____ You should count on me being late again.

First of all, if Johnny posts Mom's note (addressed to *him*), he can't say he didn't know about the dinner at the Smiths'. Pleading ignorance is made more difficult. Since much defiant behavior is "sneaky" rather than openly blatant, he's unlikely to announce he will be late. That leaves only one option.

A simpler approach could be a verbal statement that might go something like this:

Remember, Johnny, we're all going over to the Smiths' tonight at 7:00 pm. Do you think that's something you'll forget?

Verbal approaches are a bit riskier but, in this case, Johnny might indicate he won't forget. If he thinks he *could* forget, it might be helpful to work with him on a way to remember.

Letter from a chore: This one is both provocative and fun. Mary comes home from school and sees a letter on the kitchen bar. It's addressed to her in a rather unusual script. She opens it and reads.

Dear Mary:
Please help me! I'm sitting here in the closet. It's DARK and lonely in here. Mary, I haven't had any real exercise or companionship in a long, long time.

Before you start on your homework, would you take me out of the closet and run me over the carpet in the den? Please, Mary? Would you help me?

VICTOR, the Vacuum

"Great Job:" I've been sharing this idea with educators for years. (In fact, I shared a dialog-based version of this intervention back in Chapter Six; compliance-based alternatives to behavior modification were being considered.) A teacher once shared how she puts her students to a task, then, before they have little more than a heading on their papers, she writes "Great Job!!" and her initials on two or three students' work.

Students are at first surprised she would write such a thing on a blank paper, but they *like* it! Her positive comments "provoke" them into better performance.

Over the course of a week she does this with every student. "It's not a perfect intervention," she shares, "but it is an effective and encouraging gesture. I continue to use it on a regular basis."

Gift-wrap it: A school psychologist recently shared about a situation she had experienced with a student. The girl, a third grader, had caused a considerable stir with some acting out behavior at school.

A day or so later, the school psychologist went by the girl's classroom to call her out for a visit. As soon as the girl recognized the school psychologist, she took off.

(Most kids, as uncomfortable as they might be in this circumstance, would not run off. Interpretation: This girl's behavior is diagnostically quite significant.)

As you can imagine, this troubled the school psychologist. Folks don't get into this profession to scare kids away.

We spoke about the girl's embarrassment over the previous episode of her behavior, plus her likely feeling that this session was going to be uncomfortable, an accounting for the earlier episode. Working with this girl would involve "repackaging" the school psychologist's visit with her in a more positive way.

Here's what we came up with. The school psychologist would wrap a good-sized box like a colorful present and carry it with her when she picks up the girl at her classroom. (Since the school psychologist would be carrying the package with both hands, the girl could not misinterpret any gestures.) The package would contain some sort of fun activity they could do together in the psychologist's office. Little would be discussed except for the activity itself, and the visit would be kept short.

The point of this visit would be for the girl to return to her classroom following a positive experience with the school psychologist. An even better goal of this first visit after the episode would be a positive, longer, and effective *second* visit. A provocative approach (the brightly wrapped package) would help it happen. (Obviously, the inappropriate episode eventually would need to be addressed as the psychologist develops the rapport to support it.)

What Needs to Happen?

"Spit in the Soup" interventions aren't always easy to visualize and implement. They require the ability to see in a situation a way inappropriate behavior can be stopped *before* it begins. Critical to this ability is the management of one's frustration over the behavior. It's difficult, indeed, to change an approach to behavior when the adult is soaking in the problem still. Interventions do come, however, when we apply focus and practice.

There is one word of caution. It's very easy for sarcasm to slip into an intervention when a youngster's behavior is getting the better of an adult. Guard against sarcasm, as it only creates more problems.

Chapter Eighteen

Fixing the "Where"

"Where" a behavior happens and "where" we address it can also make a substantial difference. None of us float around in an undefined ether. Anything a human being does or can do *must* happen somewhere. It's yet another application of one rock-solid way to evaluate real estate: Location, location, location. "Where" matters.

Room-to-Room Tantrum

I remember a video from a television show that featured clips of people doing some strange, spontaneous, and always hilarious things. One clip was of a very young boy who was so angry at his mother he fell to the floor and pitched a Class A temper tantrum. She simply left the child there on the floor and quietly slipped into another room.

The tantrum immediately stopped as the boy got to his feet and searched every room in the house until he found Mom. As he saw her, he immediately plopped down on the floor and resumed his tantrum.

It was hysterical. The lad wasn't about to waste all that energy and effort in the *wrong* place. An audience was required, so he shifted the location (the "where") of his tirade accordingly.

Wrong-way Stones

Let's revisit our five-chapter analogy, the deck in my back yard. What if, while half asleep, I was to walk out to the deck on a foggy morning. My feet follow the stepping stones without much direction from me.

Something's wrong. I reach the last stepping stone and step up to the deck, but it's not there! On this morning the stepping stones have taken me to a dead-end. I can't see the deck anywhere.

I am temporarily lost and completely confused. After all, it was here yesterday. My morning writing ritual is interrupted as I try to locate the deck in the thickness of the morning fog.

The deck is there, somewhere, but someone has gone to a lot of trouble to rearrange all the stepping stones in the *wrong* direction. Result: My project is shoved to the back burner while I search for my favorite writing spot.

"Where" Matters (a LOT!)

Sometimes the "where" of a poor behavior, the location of its occurrence, says it all, or certainly most of it. "Where" and behavior are strongly connected into a pattern that frustrates adults to the max. "Where" becomes a huge neon sign that blinks out boldly to the youngster: "Do it *here*!" Let's consider a few rather classic examples. (All of these actually happened.)

The crayon dropper: There's a first-grader in Mrs. Smith's class who appears to delight in "accidentally" dropping all of his crayons right smack in front of the doorway at the most inappropriate moment. It always seems to happen when the teacher alerts the students to put away their art supplies and line up for lunch.

The boy says it's an accident, but this accident is amazingly predictable.

Where he drops his crayons makes all the difference, doesn't it? It's no coincidence he does his number at the only door in and out of the classroom; he's getting a payoff of some sort. (Avoidance of the cafeteria or special delight in controlling and aggravating others are two pretty powerful payoffs we'll consider in Chapter Twenty.)

The boy is fairly certain his teacher isn't going to let classmates stomp on the crayons as they head to lunch. There's going to be a delay, a delay he has orchestrated perfectly.

It wouldn't be the same, would it, if the teacher were to give him a baggie or a pail with a lid for his crayons? If he dropped the crayons in the *back* of the classroom, it wouldn't hold up lunch, so that option is out. For this kid, there's only *one* spot on this earth that'll make the perfect "where" for his crayons.

The arm bruiser: Another young man would hurry through breakfast at school so he could walk around the cafeteria and say hello to his friends. It was a painful greeting, however. He would punctuate each hello with a vigorous pop on the victim's arm. He wasn't a bad kid at all, but it soon got to where classmates would scatter when they saw him coming.

How would you deal with this behavior?

The sleepy head: A mother and father contacted me for a consultation regarding a problem that had them baffled. Their 12-year-old daughter was completely resistant to getting out of bed on school mornings. The parents would set all kinds of loud alarms, play loud music, turn on all the lights and even jerk the covers off her bed. She continued to sleep (or so it appeared) while all this was going on.

They were at their wits' end. The girl's behavior was affecting everyone.

The missing rider: Houseparents at a group home shared this interesting and irritating scenario. They operated a cottage full of adolescent girls. (There's your first clue.)

Whenever the cottage would go to town, to church, or on a fun outing, everyone would pile into the van. Well, *almost* everyone. Invariably, one girl would not be in the van, or she would run back into the house for something. This delay could go on and on. It got to the point where the houseparents seriously considered shutting down all but the most necessary trips.

What Needs to Happen?

The whole issue of discerning the "where" of behavior and managing it is not at all obvious sometimes. One has to step out of the pattern to catch it. The aim here is to arrive at ways to make the location of the intervention work in the adult's favor.

Remember back in Chapter Seven where Mom and Tommy had the discussion about feeding the dog? Where did Mom suggest putting the remote control to the television? Under the dog's bowl, right? Now *that's* a creative and supportive "where" intervention.

The painful side of "where": There can be a strong emotional connection between the "where" and the behavior, and it's not always pleasant. If a youngster was always disciplined out behind the barn, wouldn't stepping back there even years later feel like a spanking? The seat of the pants has a great memory.

This notion of painful locations is precisely why I don't know-ingly do therapy with a youngster in a place that makes them un-comfortable, unless, of course, I *want* to make them uncomfort-able for a therapeutic or disciplinary reason. Think about it; there's a very good reason why a judge has a special, elevated "where" in the courtroom.

Proactive change of "where": The proactive change of location as a component of intervention can break the old pat-terns and cycles of behavior that create the trouble. The differ-ence this simple intervention can make truly is amazing.

Let's consider the interventions that were employed with each of our four examples.

The crayon dropper: The easiest way to stop a poor behavior is to empower the child *out* of it. (You can try punitive measures and consequences, but beware. This kid generally can find a way to make you pay.)

Before the teacher announces preparations for lunch, she takes the crayon dropper to the back of the class and offers him a job with a "where": Cubby Captain. It will be his "job" to let her know when *all* the crayons are in the cubbies. Since that includes *his* crayons also, there won't be crayons on the floor.

Does that mean this youngster's behavior has been completely solved? No; it only means you have stopped crayons from hitting the floor on *that* day. Typically, however, youngsters love having a "job" with status. It's a redirection that has a chance of sustain-ing itself.

The arm bruiser: The principal at this school also em-powered this student out of the inappropriate behavior by offer-ing him a "where" job.

She suggested to him that, as he finished his breakfast, she'd like for him to take over the duty of opening and closing the cafeteria door for students who were still coming in from the buses. She noted how they often had their hands full of books and musical instruments, so having someone at the door would be a very good thing. She added one further instruction: "Whatever you do, don't turn loose of the door."

How could he hit anyone? His hitting hand stayed on the doorknob! He loved this job so much the principal shared the boy started eating breakfast at home, just so he could go straight to his door job as soon as he got to school. And the thanks he received from students coming in to breakfast was positive and powerful in affirming him and his job.

An additional intervention would be to suggest to him there are better ways to greet classmates. A little role-play wouldn't hurt, either.

(Using both interventions, the job at the door and practice on better ways to greet friends, would be a perfect example of a tactical strategy supported by a strategic intervention.)

The sleepy head: The girl's parents were really frustrated. Her behavior was even causing them trouble in their work. I explained to them how all of the circumstances of her being in bed and people trying to wake her was way too "comfortable" for her.

I suggested the girl sleep in some other part of the house, the more unconventional (and uncomfortable), the better. We discussed places like the kitchen, the laundry room, and even the garage. When she could wake up appropriately for three or four days in a row, she could go back to sleeping in her own bed, so long as the old problems didn't come back.

They seemed excited about trying a different "where." I told them to call me back if it didn't work. I never heard from them after that.

The missing rider: In this case, I noticed how the distance from the front door to the van was short, just a few steps. It was "convenient" for the girl to fall behind, ask the others to wait, or simply switch to slow-motion when it would suit her.

I suggested the houseparents park the van at least a half-block from the cottage, then walk the girls to the van in one group. I'm sure they thought the housepop was nuts, but the idea did produce some much-needed improvement.

Another idea, and this one might sound a bit strange, would have been for the houseparents to take the girls out of the cottage by a different door. Rationale: This alternative wouldn't "feel" as comfortable because elements of the old behavior patterns would not be there. It would present a better chance to start fresh. (Better yet, the housepop could park the van half a block away *and* take the girls out by a different door.)

Chapter Nineteen

Fixing the "When"

I once read an article that spoke volumes to the power of attending to "when." It was about a New York state car owner, Irv Gorden. At the time of the article, Irv had logged well over two and a half million miles on his 1966 Volvo P1800S. His secret was really no secret at all: regularly scheduled maintenance and proactive care of the vehicle.

In other words, Irv fixed problems long before they had a chance to happen.

Attention to Prevention

Our efforts at working with difficult young people shouldn't be much different than Irv's. Intervention that occurs *after* a major mechanical breakdown or a behavioral episode is expensive and stressful.

Consider that thought for a moment. It costs *plenty* in terms of effort, energy, and damaged relationships to address behavior after it's in our face. Who really *wants* to absorb the heat of a difficult youngster's reaction to an imposed consequence? Is it worth the arguing, yelling, name-calling, anger, and strain if there's another, better way to address problems?

Figure 19-1 shows how dealing with a behavior after the fact can turn stress-free moments into stress-filled ones quickly. (Sometimes we have no real choice, especially if the behavior catches us by surprise. Even then, the resulting unpleasantness is much the same.)

Figure 19-1

Bottom line: If we can intervene *before* there's an episode, just like Irv with his 46-year-old Volvo, a lot of grief could be spared.

Fixing the "when" essentially amounts to prevention, and all prevention starts with predictability. If we know what a youngster is *about* to do, we should focus on getting out in front of it. With most skills, proactive intervention (prevention) gets even better with practice. Figure 19-2 shows how getting out in front of a behavior can spare some grief.

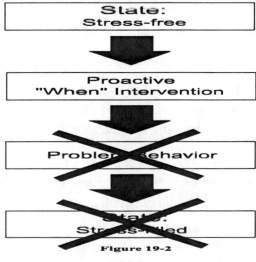

Figure 19-2

215

More Insight Than Skill

It's true; effective management of "whens" of behavior clearly requires more insight than skill. Good intervention means one is not completely comfortable when there is no trouble. (That's an interesting notion, isn't it?) After all, "stress-free" is the state of every situation just before a bad behavior erupts. (Remember, we're talking about *predictable* behavior here.)

Having a plan and implementing it at a moment when it is not needed sounds a bit strange. But that's precisely the case with good "when" management. It's too easy to get caught up in a dance you don't like after the music starts. It's another thing entirely to bring your own band.

Back to the Crayon Dropper

Consider the crayon-dropping behavior of our young student in the last chapter. We'll call him Mark. When the teacher asks the students to put away their art supplies and line up for lunch, Mark always finds a way to drop his crayons, usually right smack in front of the only door in and out of that classroom. Result: Everyone is upset, and Mark has again played a very effective game of "Gotcha."

The easiest thing in the world for Mark to do is to *keep* doing it.

Let's say that after a few of these episodes the teacher begins to think, "I *knew* he was going to do that!" There's your predictability. Now it's time to work on the "when."

The simplest thing for the teacher to do is change the activity that occurs just minutes before the class goes to lunch. If Mark and the others don't have any crayons, no crayons will end up on the floor.

Admittedly, this is an oversimplified example, but it contains the complete essence of a solution that can keep things stress-free. It is very possible Mark will come up with other behaviors, but they can be dealt with tactically and strategically, also.

What Needs to Happen?

Plan all "when" interventions carefully. The strategies *will* pay off. Proactive involvement, interventions of "when," are the easiest and most effective to implement in terms of planning, effort, and results. Outcomes from "when" management are more pleasant, more desirable, and more durable over time.

Why invite trouble? If efforts spent working on the "when" of intervention can be so productive, why are there plenty of folks who will *never* attempt to get out in front of major trouble? Why, indeed? Consider these reasons why some adults will continue to answer the door on bad behavior.

1. *Their vision is clouded.* They can't focus on the forest because the trees are in the way. The most obvious insights are out of sight. This is precisely why folks can most clearly see the struggles and mistakes of others, but not their own. They can be experts at offering advice on managing kids they *don't* have to raise or teach.

2. *They want to rest and recover in the quieter moments.* Who can blame them, really? Who wants to plan and implement interventions when there isn't yet a problem? After all, isn't that the time to bind your wounds and prepare for the next battle with this kid? If you desire a "when" intervention that will work, it might just be the time for your best effort.

3. *They don't want to work that hard.* Folks who don't want to put some thought, time, and effort into a good "when" intervention will instead find themselves working vigorously on their responses to major behavioral episodes. They will *always* be one step behind what's happening, miserable about it, and exhausted. To them, Maalox cocktails are starting to taste pretty good.

4. *The don't KNOW what to do.* We have hopefully addressed some of that.

5. *They are fearful of becoming responsible.* This one is huge, although it often wears a disguise. It's a characteristic of a person who thinks or says, "If I get involved, then some of the outcome is on *me*; I could fail." Failure is always a possibility, but at least it comes after some effort to change a bad situation. Failure can have some honor to it. Trying and failing is far better than saying, "I'll just wait until *he* decides to change." If that were the case, I would advise packing a lunch. It could be a *long* wait.

All five of these reasons must be addressed if we are to plan and implement effective interventions of "when."

A "when" sandwich: All interventions, not just the "when" ones, should serve to solve problems as they repair and restore relationships. Our intent, therefore, ought to be securely wrapped in good faith.

This doesn't mean a youngster is going to like the intervention, rather there's a way and a place for the relationship to return. We'll close this chapter with a "when" intevention that does just this.

John comes home from school and is greeted at the door by Mom. She hands him a list of some chores that need to be done. John is not happy about any of it, and he lets her know. Besides, he's hungry. How can *any* kid do chores when he's starving? John complains, and complains, and complains.

Next time, Mom greets John at the door again. This time, however, she hands him a plate holding his favorite sandwich. It's generously accompanied by some great-looking homemade french fries. She also hand him a list conspicuously labeled, *"After* Sandwich Chores."

Alright, not every problem can be remedied with a sandwich, but there's something you need to know about John: It's much more difficult for him to complain when his stomach is *full*!

Chapter Twenty

Overhauling the Outcome

For purposes of our discussion here, outcomes and payoffs are one and the same. The notion is that the desire for the payoff shapes and drives a child's behavior toward a specific and desired outcome, the payoff.

We're *all* working for outcomes. We're all involved in an on-going venture to become better (happier, healthier, more prosperous) tomorrow than we are today.

In the same manner, it's possible to strive toward payoffs that are unhealthy or that create eventual pain and difficulty on the other individuals in one's life. In these instances, the overhaul or elimination of undesirable and harmful payoffs is both noble and necessary. After all, if a loved one were killing himself with drugs and alcohol, wouldn't we try to stop him?

Back to the Deck

Going back to our analogy, the deck in my back yard was the payoff of my trip out to it. It was the outcome of my walk across the stepping stones. If the deck were to be altered in a way as to make my short journey undesirable, I wouldn't make the walk at all. I would not engage in a behavior that would take me where I no longer wish to go.

As long as we're playing "What if ...?" here, let's consider ways this outcome (payoff) of a trip across the stepping stones could be changed.

1. Someone could break the deck apart and haul it off.

2. Someone could carefully dismantle the deck and leave it there as a pile of lumber.

3. Someone could burn down the deck.

4. Someone could build a tall fence around the deck so I couldn't get to it.

5. Someone could smear sticky, black grease all over the deck.

6. Someone could drop a pile of rattlesnakes onto the deck.

All of these gestures, as ridiculous as they seem, would shut down the predicted behavior, my walk out to the deck.

Two Kinds of Payoffs

There are two kinds of payoffs or outcomes. They consist of things we wish to gain and things we wish to avoid. Both are quite powerful in driving our behavior. Conversely, altering these payoffs can change behavior.

Payoffs of gain: We covered these briefly in Chapter Three. Payoffs of gain push our behavior along every day. The desire to earn a promotion at work or to complete a master's degree can cause a person to put out an enormous amount of effort. The desire for perceived gain, however, can also direct bad behavior. The gain can be either tangible or intangible.

Tangible: A child steals a cookie from the jar because he wants it. The cookie is the payoff, so long as Mom doesn't find out. Remember the kid back in Chapter Three who threatened to destroy a shoe store unless he got his baseball cleats? He made it pay, unfortunately.

Intangible: Status and power are things you cannot touch or hold in your hand, but they are extremely powerful. How often have we seen the extremes a ruler would go to, including murder, in order to remain in power?

We all need a healthy measure of power and control in our lives. Without it, we become terribly needy, desperate, and even sick. Balance is the key. When it all goes out of balance, lives and relationships are affected, often dramatically.

I clearly can still recall a young high school student; she was a client of a counselor I was supervising. She was bright and capable, but she was failing her freshman year for the second time when her father looked for help.

Her mother had died of cancer a couple of years earlier and Dad was on the road constantly in his work. The daughter lived with an aunt most of the time, and that was not going well at all. It seemed the longer and further Dad was away, the worse her behavior and school failure became.

Dad was frantic. When she began failing again in school, he pleaded with her: "Just pass! Please, just pass!" As her grades fell even more, he cut his business trips short so he could work with the school and her teachers.

She failed, anyway. The next year found Dad being even more desperate to get his daughter through the ninth grade. There were more trips to the school, and more conferences and dealmaking with her teachers. She was failing her freshman year for the second time as her father threatened and pleaded for her just to pass her classes. That was about the time he sought counseling for the two of them.

The counselor immediately saw the purpose and direction in the girl's behavior. She encouraged the youngster to express her needs to her father directly. With the support of her counselor, the daughter shared with her father what had been difficult for her to put into words.

Daddy, I love you so much. But, Daddy, there are times when I am really, really angry at you. I sometimes feel like you have abandoned me. Mom's gone, and you are away so much with your work I sometimes feel like I have lost BOTH of you. I feel like an orphan, Daddy. What do I have to do to let you know I'm still here?

It was a turning point for both of them. Things didn't get better overnight, but they both began to earnestly and effectively work on issues that had festered terribly. Pain over the loss of a wife and mother that had been put aside was experienced authentically as father and daughter reached out to each other.

Dad couldn't quit his job but, as the two of them worked on their hearts and their healing, they each set aside time to be together and to share. Things gradually improved.

Observe in this story how the girl's control over her father's blood pressure not only earned her a pound or two of flesh in exchange for her misery, her behavior actually caused him to come up to the school and focus on her. When she failed, he showed up! Why wouldn't she keep failing? But she paid quite a price for it, a price many young people seem very willing to pay.

(Although I don't believe the girl necessarily schemed to trade school compliance for a choke-hold on her father, I *do* believe her inappropriate behavior at school was strengthened when she felt his frustration resonate with hers. Again, it was an intangible sort of payoff that is all too common in the behavior of young people.)

Payoffs of avoidance: The other payoff of behavior is the avoidance of what we *don't* want or *don't* want to happen. I'm convinced there are those folks who wake up every morning motivated by what they hope to avoid.

I don't recommend it. I'm sure the following list is just the beginning on the topic of what humans will go to considerable effort to avoid, but it's not at all difficult to see where defiant behavior of young people would plug right in.

> 1. *Pain or death.* This one's rooted in survival. I wore a bulky flack jacket in the blazing heat of south Vietnam because I preferred to keep my body parts in one piece. Is it possible people will go to extremes of behavior in order to avoid a painful event? Of course, they will. (Also consider what folks will do to avoid spiritual death.)

> 2. *Punishment.* It doesn't matter how adults spell "punishment" or "consequences," young people spell those words the same: L-O-S-S. They don't like it, and they often will lie, blame, and connive to avoid it. But isn't that one big reason we pay our taxes; so the IRS won't come knocking on *our* door?

3. *Embarrassment and humiliation.* What will we do to avoid these? A lot, I suspect. (I'm reminded of the old Tex Ritter song, *High Noon.* In the song, and the movie of the same name, a young man is willing to risk making his new wife a widow rather than be regarded a coward.)

A substitute is teaching the class one morning when the readers are delivered to the classroom. The sub decides they will all read a story from the new reader, with each student sharing one paragraph aloud.

What the substitute *doesn't* know is that Robert can hardly read at all, and that he's very sensitive about that fact. Before the reading comes to him, Robert throws his reader across the room, barely missing a student's head.

He's sent to the office. The principal is perplexed because that behavior is not like Robert at all. "What happened?" she asks the boy. He explains he'd rather be known as a kid who throws a book in class than a kid who can't read.

4. *Failure.* Embarrassment and humiliation are personal, somewhat private, experiences. But failure is public record; the whole world could be watching. How many athletes have been at the point of exhaustion, yet they reached deep and grabbed something extra, not simply because they wanted to win, but because they could not bear the thought of losing?

5. *Closeness to others.* Relationships require vulnerability and effort to maintain. They also require a narrowing of one's psychological boundaries, a need to

let others in. Some folks, certainly including young people, are so uncomfortable when others get too close they do something inappropriate (often outrageous) that pushes them away to a more "comfortable" distance. It's not exactly the way to create and deepen friendships or to remain married. Everyone suffers.

All five of these are clearly skill-related. Better skills could result in better behavior.

It Gets Complicated

Outcomes and payoffs can be tricky. They are not always easily discerned, interpreted, and addressed. In other words, we can get it wrong, sometimes. Here are a few examples of how payoffs can become complicated.

1. *Multiple or "stacked" payoffs.* Sometimes there's not just a single payoff, but several. I mentioned earlier how the deck in my back yard was the payoff of my trip to it, but how about the writing projects I accomplished there (including a legitimate best-seller, by the way)? Wouldn't they *all* be payoffs?

Consider the teen who ordered his parents to leave the kitchen until he had finished cooking and eating a pizza. (And that's *exactly* what they did!) On the surface it seems like the payoff was a pizza, and it was. A more powerful payoff, however, was the domination and control over his parents. (He also created emotional distance with his behavior, a payoff of avoidance.)

2. *Disguised payoffs.* What if a youngster specifies a payoff she desires in return for appropriate behavior, then behaves completely counter to what she herself said she wanted? This drives parents crazy!

One girl agreed to pass her classes in return for a jacket she *really* wanted. A boy was promised a car if he would pass the semester. A car! Both of them seemed excited about the bargains they had made, yet *both* of them failed.

How could this happen? Could it be that the resulting frustration of the parents was a payoff in itself? Could the payoff have been the accumulation of habitually defiant behavior on a daily basis, with its own little payoffs coming a nickel and dime at a time? (I've always believed that defiant behavior has a quality that falls just short of addiction. It can drive itself!)

And finally, could failure *be* the payoff? Youngsters faced with the strain of doing well and feeling they must maintain that performance are often relieved when they fail. Failure doesn't feel very good, but at least the stress and strain are over. In other instances, failure can be a payoff to a youngster who feels incapable of success.

3. *"I Don't Have a Clue!" payoffs.* Not understanding a payoff doesn't diminish its power to drive inappropriate behavior. Coexisting conditions, like depression, anxiety, and post-traumatic stress only serve to cloud an already murky picture. After all, what does

a depressed youngster *feel* like doing? Not much. (This is precisely the reason why a comprehensive evaluation is so important.)

When we don't know what drives behavior, it's easy to come up with a completely *wrong* intervention.

What Needs to Happen?

The short answer to solution and intervention is to eliminate or at least manage the payoffs. This involves accurate identification and a plan of intervention that is as focused as we can make it. (Effective intervention also means not creating *more* payoffs as a result of the intervention.)

Shut down tangible payoffs: Period. The short term result of removing a tangible payoff could be a behavioral episode that could win an Oscar. The whole point of the threats made by the kid who wanted baseball cleats instead of school shoes was that he would ramp up his tantrum until he got what he wanted.

Why? Because it had *always* worked before. Awful behavior had gotten him a lot. When it no longer gets him what he wants (after strenuous and failed efforts to shake loose a pair of baseball cleats), there comes a point where he's not so eager to throw his hard work down the drain. We should tie a knot and hold on until he gets there. It'll be a rough trip, but worth it.

Eliminate or minimize intangible payoffs: These are "invisible" and often quite difficult to address. And, since many intangible payoffs consist of the adult's reaction to a youngster's actions, they are difficult to change.

Intangible payoffs can be part of a dysfunctional "dance," just like the Pager Pop and his son back in Chapter One. The more Dad ranted, raved, and screamed at the boy, the more affirmed the youngster became regarding who was *really* in control. With that kind of power over the old man, why would he *ever* be inclined to stop? The boy wasn't happy, but he knew how to spread his misery around.

Obviously, most cases aren't this dramatic or even this obvious. The challenge is to look at anything we say or do as a potential payoff for poor behavior, then change it.

Reduce payoffs of avoidance: As already mentioned, payoffs of avoidance are skill-related. As we help youngsters with the necessary skills (strategic interventions), behaviors of avoidance should lessen.

A child or teen won't always be excited about working on a needed skill, or even admit a skill is lacking. It's a safe bet Robert would not have thrown his reader across the classroom if he could have handled the paragraph when it came his turn. He probably wouldn't be very excited, however, about practicing the one skill that causes him so much discomfort and embarrassment. Robert's a good kid, though. He'll get there.

I wanted to skip my high school prom my junior year. I had a great excuse: I couldn't dance. Mom not only convinced me to go to the prom, she taught me a few entry-level dance moves. I made it through, barely.

We're not talking about teaching lots of skills here. Sometimes a youngster simply wants to know how to behave and what to say at a funeral. An investment of five minutes of solid guidance and support can last a lifetime.

Chapter Twenty-one

Don't Stir the Pot

In some ways, intervention with a difficult and defiant child or teen is like giving a dose of medicine. Too little of it is ineffective, but too much of it does harm.

Discipline that goes past reasonable intervention festers within the relationship and brews into bitterness. But it often starts out in small, subtle ways, fueled by frustration. Left unattended it can grow into more damage than we can imagine.

It's what I call a "stirring" of the pot.

Two Vastly Different Pictures

George befriended me during my first three years of teaching. He taught science on the bottom floor of the same wing of the middle school. An aviator in WWII, George had been captured by the Germans after his bomber was downed. He rode out a good-sized chunk of the war in a POW camp.

POWs in Germany: "That must have been a terrible experience," I said to him. His answer surprised me.

Not as bad as you might think. Of course they'd press us for any information that would help them but, for the most part, it was bearable.

Food, medicine, and blankets became scarce near the end of the war because the Germans didn't have nearly enough, not even for themselves.

The main thing was we were out of the war at that point, noncombatants. Our families got word through the Red Cross that we were alive and reasonably okay. For us the war essentially was over, so we waited. It wasn't like living at the Ritz, but it wasn't a nightmare every day, either.

POWs in Japan: Any WWII veteran of the Pacific would tell a dramatically different story. There the enemy stirred the pot with *both* hands. POWs of the Japanese often were treated with disdain and subjected to severe humiliation in addition to starvation, disease, beatings, and maltreatment that many did not survive. Any guard who showed a shred of mercy often was subject to the same treatment. Deaths of American GIs held prisoner in Japan outnumbered those in German camps 37 to 1.

(There will be some accounts that differ from these, I'm sure. The point is that, on the one hand imprisonment was considered reasonable under the circumstances. On the other hand, imprisonment plus unrelenting, painfully-inflicted punishment was not reasonable under *any* circumstances.)

One Girl's Story

I was conducting a group therapy session one day with several adolescent girls at a residential treatment center. One of them asked me a question that led into a pot-stirring story:

Don't you have a daughter our age?

Yes, I do.

What would you do if she broke a plate in the kitchen?

It depends. If it was an accident, I wouldn't do anything. I'd just ask her to clean it up. If she broke it out of carelessness, I might take it out of her allowance. Why do you ask?

I broke a plate once and my stepdad went crazy! He poured rice out of the bag onto the floor and made me kneel on it until my knees were bloody and raw.

The girl had shared a haunting example of a stirring of the pot.

The Difference: Intent

There's hardly a parent or teacher on the planet who hasn't gone overboard on discipline with a child. Their response to the child's behavior came in a moment of frustration and anger. Going overboard or stirring the pot was neither their intent nor their plan. Consequently, they make an effort to right the wrong whenever they can.

The day my respect grew even more for my father was the day we experienced a rigorous conflict. I was in high school, and I had the notion I was just about grown. (I was wrong, of course.)

I was upset and screaming at Dad about something. In the midst of my tirade, he slapped me in the face.

I was stunned. In that instant both my father and I knew his action was wrong. He had stirred the pot. I more than deserved a consequence, but not *that* one.

Later, after we had both cooled down a bit, Dad came to me and apologized. He not only admitted to me his action had been wrong, he resolved to never do it again, and he didn't. My respect for him rose into the stratosphere, and it remained there. That was the day I learned one doesn't have to be perfect to be decent.

What Needs to Happen?

Although one does not have to be perfect to be decent, one *does* need to be vulnerable and responsible.

Being vulnerable means a parent or educator truly is disturbed by the mistakes they make with young people. Don't we *need* to be upset with ourselves when we have been blatantly wrong? Although it hurts to look at those times when we have "stirred the pot," it's the vulnerability we experience that moves us to repair the relationship. When we are wrong, it *ought* to bother us. (If it doesn't, a much bigger problem exists. There is no such thing as a license to be inappropriate without accountability.)

Being responsible means taking action on our mistakes (like my father did), or taking action before a tendency becomes a mistake. It might even mean doing the "cleaning" Dr. Hew Len spoke of in Chapter Eleven, a removal of the limits that can slowly build between ourselves and our children.

Chapter Twenty-two

Mastering Noncoercive Response

A few years back I attended a workshop primarily because the title caught my attention: "Anger Control Made Easy." The training was conducted by Israel Kalman, a psychotherapist from Staten Island, New York (Kalman, 2004).

I left that program with three thoughts racing around in my head:

> 1. *Anger control is NOT easy.* Unfortunately, we tend to make it more difficult than it needs to be. (This was Kalman's point, I believe.)

> 2. *Kalman's thoughts on the matter resonated with mine.* What he shared that day easily connected with what Patterson, Shapiro, and Vance had to say about coercive loops, those typically destructive patterns of angry conflict. (We discussed this back in Chapter Seven.)

> 3. *There had to be a clear and concise way of using these interventions with young people.* Kalman presented ideas in the training that mostly applied to adult interactions, but it seemed that children and teens could benefit in powerful ways, also. They could learn to use the interventions when faced with anger-evoking challenges.

A Problem on Automatic Pilot

Part of the solution to heated and coercive struggles, especially with an oppositional and defiant youngster locked into desperate behavior, is an awareness of coercive conflict and how it can do damage all the way around.

Making Julie's day: In my live training on the subject, I often use the following dialog with an imaginary young lady, Julie. I would focus on giving participants the feel and flavor of a coercive conflict, a loop. This would be a benchmark for measuring the effectiveness of intervention.

> Doc (me): *Julie, I want you to help me demonstrate a sort of conflict between two people who are upset. For the sake of this role-play, I want you to call me a name that would upset me. For instance, you could call me an idiot. Keep in mind, Julie, that it will be my job to get you to stop calling me that. Ready? Go!*

> Julie: *You're an idiot!*

> Doc (red in the face and flustered): *WHAT? You can't call me that! It's a mean and ugly thing to call someone an idiot. You take it back right now, Julie, and don't you EVER call me an idiot again. Understand?*

Julie: *Idiot! Idiot! Idiot!*

Doc (about to explode): *But I just told you to NEVER call me that again! Never, never, NEVER!*

Julie (with some measure of glee): *Idiot! Idiot! IDIOT!!!*

Get the idea? What is it about Julie and what she's saying in this little scenario that I truly can control? Nothing; absolutely nothing! In fact, my ranting and raving is entertainment for her. All she has to do is keep throwing out that word, "Idiot!" and I'll keep the floor show moving along.

Why should she even *want* to stop?

After a bit, I begin to take on the look of *exactly* what she's calling me.

Provocative and coercive: Kids get into these sorts of conflicts all the time. They might be a bit discrete, not choosing to create a full-blown version right in front of an adult, but kids *know* which peers they can send into orbit with just a word or gesture. And, if a conflict is strong enough to cause an adult to back down, or to avoid a compliance task altogether, they'll stick with what works for them.

Doctors Patterson and Shapiro suggested that this sort of conflict typically stops when one or the other capitulates (gives in, quits, or surrenders) or resorts to some sort of physical retaliation. (What comes to mind is a junior version of a barroom brawl.) Julie couldn't very well continue to scream "Idiot!" if I knocked her unconscious, could she? But that would escalate the problem to a whole new level.

Any youngsters who initiate this cycle of conflict are being clearly provocative and coercive in their actions. It only makes sense they would be selective as to where and when they stage the fight. Since they probably wouldn't do it with another youngster when an adult is close (that would be like robbing someone in front of a cop), authority figures often are left to figure out what happened *after* the fact.

A Noncoercive Approach

At this point in my demonstration, I would switch to a different strategy, one designed to mange the "loop" (escalation of insults and tempers as each party responds) by controlling the element of coercion.

There are four parts to this intervention. We'll use a triangle to explain the parts.

Part One: *Maintain a noncoercive posture.* Here's where special effort is taken to remain unruffled and in control. As much as possible, physical cues to being upset (arms crossed, finger pointing, angry looks, etc.) are avoided. This alone will greatly reduce the coercive element in the exchange, and it will serve better to disarm the coercion of the other person.

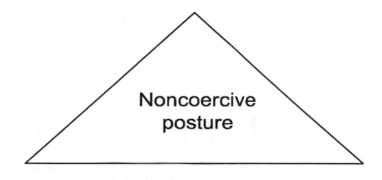

Figure 22-1

Part Two: *Objectively describe what has happened, what has started the conflict.* It is critical this description be absolutely factual and accurate to the events. It must not allow any room for misinterpretation. I tell folks it's much like having a video camera present at the conflict. What is seen and heard on the video cannot be disputed. If I were to accuse Julie of calling me an idiot, it could be verified by replaying the video. There's no material for argument.

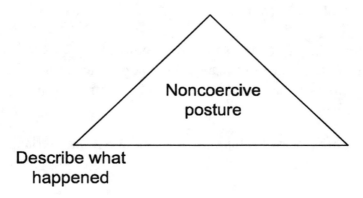

Figure 22-2

Conversely, if I were to reply, "Julie, you must think I'm a hateful, awful person," I've stepped away from objectivity and into mind reading. In doing so, I've also opened the door for disagreement and more conflict.

I find young people are very perceptive as to what is an objective response to provocation and what is not. Here are a few examples to use as practice. Let youngsters come up with others; they'll love it.

You just bumped me out of this line. (objective)

You're crazy! (true perhaps, but *not* objective)

You just spit on me! (objective)

You're a yellow-livered liar! (a jaundiced opinion, but *not* objective without an autopsy)

Your mama wears combat boots! (provocative, but probably *not* objective)

Part Three: *Express your vulnerability.* This is an appeal to the goodness of a usually appropriate relationship. It reaches across the conflict to say, "What you did and said hurt me. If you care, you'll want to work this out." (This is precisely why this intervention *won't* work very well if the individuals already have ongoing friction between them.)

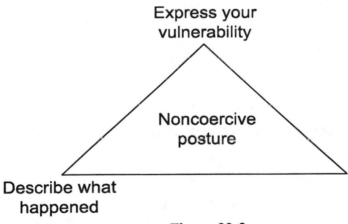

Figure 22-3

This approach won't work if the other party doesn't care about resolving the conflict. Surprisingly, it works best with total strangers. Reason: We tend to be on our best behavior with people we don't know at all, while we'll show our poorest behavior with those we know well, such as family members.

239

Some folks get stuck in this vulnerability part. They view vulnerability as a sign of weakness. (In some cases, such as all-out war, or life or death struggle, it *would* be a weakness.)

It's easy for folks to misunderstand vulnerability and how it is expressed. As I was explaining this part of the intervention to one school principal, he became visibly concerned.

Principal: *I'm not at all certain I want a disruptive student knowing I'm vulnerable.*

Doc (me): *Two things. First, what you just said is a statement of vulnerability, a very appropriate one. Second, does it concern you when a student's behavior threatens the welfare of all the others?*

Of course.

Sure; it does. So what would be the problem in telling that student something like, "I take my job here very seriously. It bothers me, it bothers me a lot, when ANY student does something that affects the safety and welfare of the others"?

I wouldn't have a problem with that at all. I've said it, or something similar, plenty of times. It's true.

That would be a statement of vulnerability.

Is it possible that vulnerability can be overstated? Absolutely. In stating vulnerability, it's not necessary to tearfully express how much sleep you're losing over the problem, that you're now seeing a psychiatrist, that you've had to increase your blood pressure medication, or that your Maalox cocktails are now all doubles.

Part Four: *Probe for the problem.* In this part of the intervention the task is to focus on the issue that fueled the conflict in the first place.

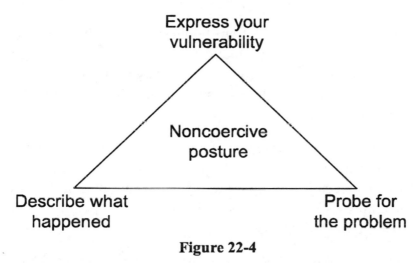

Figure 22-4

In the case of the example with Julie, her behavior of calling me an idiot didn't happen because she had a sudden revelation. It likely happened because I made her angry in some way. This is the primary issue, but it's often overlooked. (As we've seen, it's also possible a youngster will start a loop and keep it going as a way of avoiding the issue entirely.)

If I were to focus on what prompted Julie to call me an idiot, the issue might be resolved. If it were a conflict between two youngsters, it's very possible adults would address the ensuing fight over name-calling, but not the deeper concern or issue. This is precisely how problems fester and accumulate unresolved.

At this point in the intervention a simple statement might open the opportunity for a deeper look.

> *What has happened or what have I said or*
> *done that would cause you to call me an idiot?*

The response to this question should start some dialog capable of resolving the deeper problem, if both parties are willing to participate (not always a given). Obviously, if I probed for the problem and discovered I was responsible, I should own up to it as a part of the resolution.

This part of the intervention should conclude with a statement like, "Is there *anything* else we need to work through or talk about?" The idea is to keep asking this question until the answer is something like, "No, I guess that's it." At that point, the conflict should be extinguished.

(A thought: Wouldn't the marriage relationship work much better if both partners used this approach to resolve conflicts? Don't think for a minute this information is for young people only.)

Of course, conflict isn't always resolved smoothly, but an approach like this one is *much* better than a trip to Fist City, with the *real* problem still smoldering on the table.

Julie, again: At this point in my demonstration, I would offer a different dialog with Julie, one which contained all the parts of this intervention.

Doc: *Let's try this again, Julie. I want you to start it off exactly the same way as before. This time, however, I'm going to respond differently. Again, my job is to see if I can get you to stop. Ready? Go!*

Julie (with gusto): *You're an idiot!*

Doc (concerned, but in control): *Julie, you just called me an idiot.*

Julie: *Yes; I did. IDIOT!*

Doc: *That's what I thought you said. Julie, I don't like being called that, and I can't imagine anyone who would. It hurts, Julie. What on earth has happened, or what have I said or done that would cause you to call me an idiot?*

Julie: *Well, I was at the store yesterday with my mother, and I saw you two aisles over. I smiled and waved, but you just ignored me. You acted like I was invisible. You hurt MY feelings!*

Doc: *Oh, Julie. You're right; I was at that store yesterday. But I promise; I DIDN'T see you. I guess I wasn't paying attention. Julie, if I had seen you, I would not only have waved at you, I would have walked over and said hello. But I didn't, Julie, and I'm sorry for that. It was not my intent to hurt you in any way. Is there anything else we need to work out while we're talking about it?*

Julie: *No, I guess not. That was it.*

In this example, Julie did not bring up any other issues. If she had, I would have handled them, one at a time, in a similar fashion.

None of this is rocket science. There can be some bumps in the road. They usually occur when the coercive stuff kicks in and stirs up old behavior patterns.

Benefits of this Approach

Why would a youngster be encouraged to try this noncoercive approach to conflict resolution, especially if the physical expression of anger has some pretty powerful payoffs of it's own? Consider these benefits.

1. *It represents the high road.* Noncoercive response to conflict is a more sophisticated approach to dealing with life's problems. As such, it can offer powerful benefits as youngsters move into adulthood. (It's also a skill that can help one move up quickly in the company, a skill that can be taken to the bank.)

Whenever you explain to youngsters what "sophisticated" means, they *all* want some of it. (In my opinion, the only reasons why any person, child or adult, would *deliberately* choose to be mean and unsophisticated would be because they don't know a better way to respond, or they feel permanently stuck with their current behavior.

2. *It puts the youngster in the driver's seat.* Who *doesn't* want to be in charge of outcomes? The person who can control the coercion in a conflict generally controls and directs how it works out. That has to feel good.

3. *They won't have to experience negative consequences for poor behavior.* In other words, they avoid a great deal of discomfort and pain. (No pain also feels good.)

4. *They are viewed as problem solvers rather than problem starters.* What would be the value of that in terms of a changed perspective of this youngster?

5. *All of their relationships improve.* In a world that values the capacity of an individual to get along with others, this one can carry a person far.

What Needs to Happen?

As you share this triangle approach to noncoercive response with young people, strive to do more than just teach it. Role-play it with them until they are comfortable with the steps and the process. Next, encourage them to try it in real life situations and report back with the results. It's a powerful skill; it will work for them just about every time.

Bag lady: Make the effort to encourage noncoercive response by using it yourself. Work at it until it becomes a comfortable habit.

I remember using the process one morning at an airline ticket counter. When it came my turn to check my bag, the agent was rather sharp and stern with me. (Two people directly in front of me had received the same treatment.) Taken back by this rude behavior, I decided to practice the stuff I had been teaching.

> *It seems to me you're being rather short and brisk with me this morning. It* does *make me uncomfortable. Have I done something wrong or inappropriate to offend you while I've been waiting in this line?*

(Notice how, with practice, it doesn't take long to go all the way around the triangle with this response.)

Her face softened immediately.

> *Oh, no sir. It's nothing you have done. I DO apologize. I had to put my mother in a nursing home last night. To be honest, it's really eating on me this morning. Again, I am sorry. Let me get you on your way.*

In sharing this story with young people, I would ask them to contrast this approach to one where I instead became very angry at the agent and insisted on complaining to her supervisor and the airline. Which one would have worked out better? (Had I intimidated her, she could have pushed the panic button and called TSA in a heartbeat. My destination for that morning would not have mattered, as *my* seat on that flight would have been empty.)

It would help for us all to remember we're not the only folks who experience difficulty along the way.

Ride the high road: It's great to take the high road, but it's even better when someone takes it with you. Did you ever take a defective item back to the store expecting a hassle in getting a replacement or refund? Yet when you got to the customer service desk, the clerk was empathetic, cooperative, and understanding. What happened? Could you *stay* angry and upset? Probably not. The experience possibly even made you a more loyal customer of that store.

Third-party intervention: It never occurred to me I could use this noncoercive intervention as a third-party participant, an observer. The inspiration came while I was on a cross-country flight with my nine-year-old grandson.

Jake had never flown before. He was nervous. His hands and knees kept bumping the back of the seat in front of him. I checked my impulse to give the boy a grandpa lecture about this annoying behavior. I took a different approach:

(Whispering) *Jake, I've been noticing how you've been banging and bumping into the back of that seat with your hands and knees. There's a person sitting in that seat. They probably feel every bump and bang. That can't make them very happy. Do you know how to fix that?*

He nodded, and the banging and bumping stopped immediately. The issue was over and solved.

Consider how you might use and share a third-party approach to noncoercive response.

Chapter Twenty-three

Resolving Conflicts with Your Children

Editor's Note: This chapter was part of the promotion of this book. It was written as a short ebook, *Resolving Conflicts with Your Children*. Since this book, *The Changing Behavior Book*, is already in your hands right now, the conclusion of this chapter has been revised to fit our "What Needs to Happen?" theme.

Response to the ebook was quite encouraging. One grandmother shared how she followed the book's ten steps to address conflict she was having with her adolescent granddaughter. "It was better than six months of counseling," she shared.

The reader will note how this chapter incorporates ideas, concepts, and interventions discussed in earlier chapters.

As long as there are parents and children, or teachers and students, there will be conflict. It's a component of relationships from time to time.

Conflict isn't always a bad thing; sometimes it's necessary. Otherwise, all children would grow up so self-centered and egotistical they wouldn't be able even to stand themselves.

No, we don't want to eliminate conflict. What we want to eliminate is the damage of mismanaged conflict.

Conflict and Survival

Conflict occurs when each person in the conflict wants to win. As a concept, the need to win began as a biological imperative. Early on, winning was more than a lofty goal or a good idea.

When early man crawled out of his cave each morning, he could not afford to lose even once. Survival depended on it, and you'd better believe it was etched on every fiber in the gene pool.

Enter the victim: But, even then, winning produced an interesting by-product: a victim. Victims back then, however, weren't much of a problem because they didn't last long. They were eaten quickly. The victim problem was absorbed in the process of survival. If you were still alive at the end of the day, you *were* the winner. Keeping score was not difficult.

This isn't true today, is it? Victims can hang around for decades, giving their hurt, pain, embarrassment, and frustration years to boil and fester. The accumulation of negative experiences and bad memories handicaps these folks in life and steals their joy. The victim issue is, in my opinion, the absolute root of much misery, disease, divorce, and even death in our world today.

Change is needed: Unfortunately, typical avenues for helping victimized individuals get past life-limiting issues have, on balance, been less than successful. This is nothing new; we've known it for years. What is new, at least to me, is a change in our perception of the problem.

Can a change in perception really make a difference? It can make *all* the difference.

Epiphany

Have you ever had an epiphany, an instant when everything became crystal-clear to you? I'm talking about an instant when answers to years of questions fell squarely into your lap unannounced? This is exactly what happened to me on a trip to California a few summers back. Someone I didn't know showed me how to connect the dots on a picture that to me had always been incomplete. It was a picture of the potential to heal hurting young people at a level of almost 100%.

As the picture and how to share it with others became clear to me, I could hardly wait to get back home and dive head-first into this new and invigorating project. It is, without question, the most meaningful thing I have written in 30 years. What you are reading now is but a small part of the larger work.

Looking in a different place: My summer epiphany might have been a miracle to me only, but it did cause me to look at all the well-intending mistakes I made in the past as an educator, psychologist and, yes, as a father. What I learned caused me to stop looking out *there* for the problem, but rather to look *inside* for the solution.

That's a pretty radical approach, huh? Well, it works. Consider how this approach works with marvelous consistency in one of the most solid models of healing you'll ever find: the Twelve Steps of Alcoholics Anonymous.

A different approach to healing: Consider the work of Hawaiian psychologist, Dr. Ihaleakala Hew Len. In the 1980s he put into motion the healing of a whole ward of criminally insane patients, not by working on them, but by working on himself.

Was he successful? From what I have learned, all the patients except two were healed to the point the ward was closed.

On the surface this story seems difficult to believe, but consider how this approach really isn't that farfetched at all. Whenever we change, and I'm talking about life-altering, cleansing change, others will change also. They *must* change; they cannot remain the same.

Demolition Derby

When I was a kid, Dad and my uncle Ray loved to go to the stock car races. Since I was the oldest grandchild by several years, I had the honor of tagging along.

These were dirt-track events. This meant that, if you sat close to the track, some of that dirt would end up on *you*! That was pretty cool stuff for this nine-year-old.

My favorite event was the Demolition Derby. (They still have them today, usually as a stand-alone event at county fairs.) Contestants would pile into junker cars and make it their goal to be the last car still capable of moving.

It was a *hoot*! Cars would go ramming into one another, each one trying to deliver a blow that would disable the other (the radiator was the bull's-eye). It was conflict on a grand scale.

Or was it? When the Demolition Derby was over, all the drivers would pile into the one car still running and head for the local watering hole for a few beers and a bunch of stories.

It wasn't conflict; it was entertainment. And everyone knew it. In real life, however, conflict can put human beings out of commission *permanently*.

Coercion and Conflict

A person's need to win can include the need to cajole, coerce, or otherwise overpower anyone or anything in their way. In fact, the coercive component of conflict is so predictable in its course that Dr. Gerald Patterson of the University of Oregon has a name for it: The Coercive Process. (I've never met Dr. Patterson, but I did spend a day with Dr. Jeremy Shapiro, a clinical psychologist with Case Western Reserve University in Cleveland. Dr. Shapiro is quite knowledgeable of Dr. Patterson's work.)

Looped conflict: The Coercive Process, sometimes called The Coercive Loop, is operating whenever two individuals become so disagreeable with one another that the response of one adds fuel and more negativity to the response of the other. From there it escalates until one of them either capitulates or shoves the other into compliance using force. It's also possible a bright and difficult youngster skillfully can use the power of the loop to *avoid* complying.

Here's an example of a coercive process involving a married couple.

> Wife: *Tell me, why are you so mean and hateful all the time? I'd like to know.*

> Husband: *Well, I reckon anyone married to you would turn out mean and hateful sooner or later.*

The good news about this little scenario is that both of them are adults (well, sort of), fairly capable of taking care of themselves in the conflict.

A gut-level solution: I knew of a couple who would get into massive conflicts on a regular basis. The husband developed a stress-related colon condition which, when in episode, required hospitalization and a *lot* of expense. It got to the point where he only had look to like he was getting sick during an argument and the wife would shut down completely. He controlled it all, with his *gut*!

But what happens when the coercive process starts boiling between a frustrated adult and an irresponsible youngster? Exactly how does a kid manage to hold his own against the size, power, resources, and demands of the adult?

He doesn't, not directly anyway. That would be way too dangerous and risky. But the youngster gets in his shots in other ways: passive-aggressive behavior, forgetfulness, "silent" oppositionality and defiance, and the big one of noncompliance.

A kid with a plan: I knew a pre-teen who would poop his pants whenever his stepmother would push a confrontation into painful conflict. Although that behavior sent her into orbit, it also brought the discussion to a rapid close! It was a perfect example of a full-blown coercive loop the kid learned to control to perfection. The boy's behavior was hard on the relationship, but it was highly effective in closing a conflict quickly.

Any variety of these reactive behaviors brought youngsters to my office. They were precisely the reason why subsequent conflict happened and kept on happening. It became a vicious cycle, a cycle that, too often, the youngster had learned to control.

Resolving Conflict

The secret to resolving negative conflict with a youngster is to remove coercive elements and manage it as a problem-solving discussion. It's also important to understand that *resolving* the conflict is better than *winning* the conflict because there doesn't have to be a loser, a victim. We're going to cover the process of this confrontation step-by-step. (I'm not wild about describing this process as "confrontation," but it's the closest word that fits.)

The steps for resolving conflict require the adult and the youngster to be rational, focused, and comfortable enough to participate. These steps are intended to be supportive and noncoercive as solutions to problems are sought.

> 1. *Approach the situation as if every problem was YOUR fault.* Although that might not be the case, coming to the confrontation from a position of 100% responsibility can change you in a way that is not only positive, but cleansing and effective beyond belief. At the very least, taking responsibility manages *your* anger and frustration. It positions you as a player in the discussion rather than an accuser and, perhaps for the first time, it will open the ears and the mind of the youngster. Remember Dr. Hew Len's success with the criminally insane patients? This is how he approached his work with them.
>
> Considering the severity of his patients, what else *could* he change other than himself? Criminally insane patients aren't exactly adept at managing a conversation or a relationship. In comparison, any work we would do with reasonably intact children and adolescents ought to be a dream.
>
> (If this approach bothers you a bit, congratulations. You're normal; it bothered me, too. Just keep in mind that, as the youngster later offers you his take on the problems at hand and suggests solutions, he will then become responsible for acting on the solutions *he* suggests.)

2. *Remember, your children and students DON'T hate you.* Kids can and will say some terrible and cutting things when they are upset, but they rarely mean them with permanence. In all my years of working with young people and their families, I've encountered less than a handful of youngsters who didn't genuinely care about their relationships with parents and teachers. Anger and frustration can cloud things a lot but, beneath it all, an element of caring is almost always there.

3. *Slow down, a LOT.* Speed is the enemy of reason and effective, empowered solutions. If you have to do anything quickly, the results often will be less than optimal. If this discussion, this positive confrontation, is to be effective, it can't be rushed. The path to authentic healing is a *slow* path. (With our high-octane lifestyles, slowing down just might be one of the biggest challenges to the whole intervention process.)

4. *Be sensitive to the "where" of the confrontation.* Physical locations often arouse rough and troubling memories of what happened earlier in that place. It can be a mental and an emotional obstacle for both of you. It's important to move the confrontation to a more neutral location, a place not associated with any prior difficulty.

5. *Be physically and emotionally relaxed as you open the confrontation.* Body language is a powerful transmitter of what's coming. Keep it conversational and noncoercive. I've had success talking with youngsters as we took a short walk. There's something about movement that makes the process work better. If you're seeing the child or adolescent at school, however, confidentiality might limit your mobility.

6. *Open the confrontation with an objective statement of fact.* Don't infer anything that can't be observed or documented. Describing the child's behavior should be like describing a photograph or a video. This is so critical because, if the confrontation includes too much inferred content ("You just don't care about doing *anything* to help out around this house"), you'll probably lose the youngster. Besides, you don't really know what's going on inside her head, anyway.

Although the facts are confrontational, they are, after all, still the facts. Here's an opener coming from a father to a son:

Todd, two weeks ago you told me that every Wednesday morning before you left for school, you'd bring the garbage bin around to the front so it can be emptied. I checked the bin when I came in this afternoon. It's still in the back, and it's full.

Todd might have some reasons why the garbage wasn't taken around front that morning, but he'd have a hard time arguing the location and the state of the bin at that moment. Just focus on the facts (like Sergeant Joe Friday did in every episode of the old TV series, *Dragnet*).

You can even use this approach to confront an earlier outburst from the youngster. Remember to keep it descriptive and factual. Here a mother speaks to her daughter:

Marcy, when you left for school this morning you screamed, "I wish you weren't my mother," and slammed the door behind you.

At this point it's possible that one or both of these youngsters might attempt to offer an apology or even go and fix the problem right then. It's important, however, to redirect them back to the discussion so there won't be any interruption in the steps.

A teacher might state a positive confrontation like this. Notice how it remains descriptive and factual, as if the teacher is narrating a video of the youngster's behavior.

John, I have noticed that when I give out an assignment, you frown and look upset. I've also noticed those assignments don't get finished and turned in.

7. *State your vulnerability.* This step might seem a bit surprising, but the admission of vulnerability is considered a prized commodity in good, working relationships. (Besides, if we get upset at the child, become red in the face, and start raising our voices, that's *also* an expression of vulnerability, but it's the sort of expression that can reinforce or pay off the behaviors we *don't* want.) An appropriate expression of vulnerability from the adult is an indirect appeal to the youngster to fix the problem and help restore the relationship.

Vulnerability might be stated in the following ways, using the same scenarios as before. Notice how these statements are meant to pull the child into a position of responsibility without sounding too much like a lecture.

(Dad speaking to Todd) *It concerns me that we have to keep all that garbage in our back yard for another week, while we keep adding to it. It's unhealthy for our family, Todd, and that scares me some.*

(Mom to Marcy) *I was hurt by what you said, Marcy. There is no job or role I have that means more to me than being your mother.*

(Teacher to John) *It frustrates me, John, when I see a student of mine get further and further behind. It concerns me a lot.*

8. *Probe for the problem.* In this phase of the confrontation, we ask the youngster for her take on the issue or problem that has been described.

This can require patience, as a first answer might be, "I don't know." (A counselor friend of mine was fond of saying at this point, "Yes, but if you *did* know, what would the answer be?")

If little or nothing comes from the youngster, suggest that you'll give her some time to think it over while you're still sitting with her. If the wait and the silence start to become uncomfortable, that's good. There's a good chance you'll get an answer of some kind.

If the youngster still can't come up with anything, suggest the need to schedule another meeting. It's amazing how insight suddenly arrives to a youngster when she's faced with the possibility of *another* meeting.

It is critical, of course, to probe for the problem without being overly accusatory in the process, or by asking questions that "lead" the youngster to the problem and solution *you* want to address. (A youngster might agree that your suggested problem is the issue, but if she really doesn't believe it, she won't put much effort into the solution.)

Here's some sample dialog using our three examples.

(Dad to Todd) *What's the problem here, Todd, and how can we fix it? I REALLY want to know.*

(Mom to Marcy) *Help me understand. What was that about? Marcy, I don't want for either of us to go through that again. What do you suggest we do?*

(Teacher to John) *John, what do you see as the problem here? How can we work this out so you don't fail this class?*

9. *Extinguish the problem.* This happens in two ways. First of all, problems are probed so they *can* be fixed. Start by working with the information the youngster gives you. Since it's his view, he will be more willing to put effort and energy into resolving it. You both might realize it's not workable, but there's a decent chance that a joint plan can be developed. Make the solving of the problem or issue as win/win as you can, and comment on the effort the youngster puts into working on it. (After all, he *wants* you to notice.)

By way of example, let's say that Todd tells Dad that he needs help remembering about trash day. Perhaps they come up with a cue, a digital photo of the garbage bin. Dad hands his son the picture the evening before (a nonverbal reminder), and Todd puts the photo on top of his school books or in some other conspicuous place. (Haven't we all needed a "reminder" once in awhile?)

Be aware that the youngster might come up with a problem that really isn't *the* problem. It might be a trial balloon. This could be due to a certain amount of fear and apprehension, or it could be a test, a way to see just how committed and authentic you are in helping to resolve the issue. That leads to a follow-up question, the second way to extinguish the problems:

Great; that's definitely something we can work on. Tell me, is there anything else? Anything at all? Are we good? Are there any other issues or problems that you can think of?

Questions delivered to extinguish the problems can be quite therapeutic because the *real* problem often bubbles to the surface after the first one is shared and discussed successfully. When the youngster says there are no other problems, he's expected to commit to fixing the ones he has mentioned.

(I worked with a 14-year-old girl who had been placed in a group home because her mother had a multitude of issues in her life, including cancer. I visited with the girl and asked her if she had any problems she needed to work on. "No, I don't," was her terse, rather indignant, response.

When our visit was over she asked me if she could go home. "Well, your mom's not ready for you to come home just yet," I explained. "She's dealing with a lot of issues right now."

"Well, I have issues, too!" the girl screamed at me. I reminded her that, just a few minutes earlier, she had told me she had no issues or problems needing attention. I then asked her which statement was true. Challenged to select either "A" or "B," she took "C" when she said, "Why are you being so MEAN to me?")

Work on any other issues or problems that surface, or set a time to do so. It wouldn't be a bad idea to have a quick conference later to check on the progress and implement appropriate changes to the plan.

10. *Thank the youngster.* This one is very important. When closing this confrontation, express your appreciation to the youngster for her efforts in helping you with the issues identified. A short follow-up note would be a great idea, also.

Headings-only List

It might help to look at the ten steps written as a headings-only list.

1. Approach the situation as if every problem was *your* fault.

2. Remember, your children and students *don't* hate you.

3. Slow down, a *lot*.

4. Be sensitive to the "where" of the confrontation.

5. Be physically and emotionally relaxed as you open the confrontation.

6. Open the confrontation with an objective statement of fact.

7. State your vulnerability.

8. Probe for the problem.

9. Extinguish the problem.

10. Thank the youngster.

Two Other Types of Confrontation

Here is a short description of two more confrontation approaches to resolving conflict.

Aha! One intervention, I call it the Aha! Confrontation, is great to use when a child or adolescent demonstrates multiple, almost identical issues of noncompliance, such as chronic bouts of missing or incomplete school work. I've been sharing it with teachers for years.

The goal here is to focus more on the solution rather than the confrontation. To do this, you make the problem tangible, so the child can actually see and touch it (such as missing assignments or issues with a report card), as you spontaneously and gently interpret the defiance and pull the youngster in as a player in resolving the problem.

Good faith: The other type of confrontation is called the Good Faith Confrontation. This approach is designed specifically for parents. It takes a tremendous amount of vulnerability and requires parents to buy into their part of the problem and act on it vigorously and quickly.

When parents actively work on their part of the problem, it makes it more difficult for the child to do nothing in return. It cuts into their excuses dramatically. It's this specific action that lays the foundation for success.

Improvement with this intervention can be measured in minutes, not weeks. There is a downside, however: Many folks aren't ready for this deep an intervention, nor is it appropriate for every situation (especially if the youngster is fearful of the parents).

What Needs to Happen?

Read and re-read the ten steps. Practice them a few times before you sit down with the youngster. Work on being relaxed and cordial as you invite her to work with you on solving specific problems. If you get stuck, or feel like you are becoming frustrated, shut it down quietly and try again at another time.

I wish you success, but I wish you much more than that. I wish you a life-lifting epiphany that will positively transform you and the young people in your life.

Chapter Twenty-four

Exercising Acceptance and Forgiveness

It's been said that a state of unforgiveness lies at the very core of many types of illness. (Pascal's comment, the one about man's problems stemming from an inability to sit quietly with himself, could pertain to unforgiveness.) In truth, unforgiveness can do more damage to the victim than to the offender.

Costly, Indeed

Unforgiveness literally can cause disease and death.

Healthy recovery is never complete if unforgiveness remains a thorn in one's collection of experiences. Unforgiveness sows confusion, lingering hurt, and bitterness that block the path to authentic happiness and healing. Unforgiving people are not happy people. For them, the past takes them to an unacceptable future.

Well-intending, but wrong: It's quite common for friends, relatives, clergy, and counselors to insist a person forgive injustices done to them. These efforts, as well-intending as they might be, typically fail for at least two reasons:

1. *Coerced forgiveness is worse than none at all.* If it looks, sounds, and feels ingenuine, no one can benefit.

2. *To rush forgiveness is to invite trouble.* Individuals become ready to forgive only after they have a solid grasp on the hurt they are forgiving. It can't be rushed, otherwise forgiveness would be hollow and without substance. Everyone has their own timetable, as experiences and interpretations are unique to the individual. To rush them through forgiveness would be like asking them to board a flight that hasn't yet landed.

Lives on hold: The best kind of forgiveness is sought authentically; the offender apologizes and asks to be forgiven by the offended. Although this leads to the best possible kind of forgiveness, it can be a rare circumstance. The reality is that most offenders *never* ask for forgiveness. For an offended person to put their life on hold waiting on an apology and a request for forgiveness is for them to become lost in the waiting.

I've personally worked with physically, sexually, and emotionally abused young people who were waiting in just this manner, waiting and wanting for the offender to take responsibility for the hurt and damage they had done. Unfortunately, many of the offenders (some in prison) either felt they did nothing wrong or they could not see past themselves enough to realize what they had inflicted upon another human being. Even the most ready-to-forgive young person has little chance to exercise forgiveness in the most authentic manner. This is why I began teaching affected young people a concept I call "the spirit of forgiveness."

The Spirit of Forgiveness

The spirit of forgiveness is very close to an actual act of forgiveness between the offender and the offended because it serves to complete the process for the offended person even if actual forgiveness is never sought.

(It's interesting to note the exact opposite can be a viable process. It might include a situation in which an offender desires forgiveness from someone who won't or can't give it, as in the case of death. The spirit of forgiveness works well in this instance, also. We'll revisit this thought at the end of this chapter.)

The process of the spirit of forgiveness isn't that complicated at all. Attention to a few simple steps can achieve much in healing.

Evaluate readiness to forgive: The process we're going to consider here checks the youngster's thinking and readiness to forgive by using a "What if ...?" scenario.

> *Tracy, what if your stepdad were to say to you, "I'm sorry for the hurt and pain I've caused you. None of it was your fault. The fault was entirely mine. I realize that now, and I'm deeply sorry for it. Will you forgive me?"*

(If you decide to try this, be aware it is *powerful* stuff.)

My experience has shown that Tracy will give one of three answers to this "What if ...?"

> *I would forgive him,* or

> *I'll NEVER forgive him,* or

> *He would NEVER say anything like that to me.*

Each one of these responses speaks volumes as to what's going on inside Tracy's head.

Narrow the options: My first task would be to eliminate the third response ("He would *never* say anything like that to me!"), if it is the one given. This brings choices down to a "yes" or "no" response.

> *Yes, Tracy, it is quite unlikely he would ever say something like that. But this is a "What if … ?" we're talking about. Let's say someone you admire and trust, someone like your grandmother, told you your stepdad was going to ask you for forgiveness. Then she told you he would be sincere, honest, truthful, and genuinely remorseful in asking. In other words, Tracy, Grandma's telling you he's being real in the asking. What would you do?*

Once in awhile a youngster might say, "I will *never* forgive him." This young person clearly is saying she's not ready to forgive. Pressing for or insisting on forgiveness at this point is harmful and unwise. (To use our previous analogy, the plane is still in the air.)

Genuine and authentic forgiveness requires that, upon forgiving, a person lays aside their anger and resentment to the fullest extent possible. A person who is unwilling or not yet ready to forgive is also unwilling or not yet ready to give up their anger.

Why is this so? They're *still* using it. An offer of more time is the preferred intervention for this youngster.

Young people are more gracious than we imagine. Most of the time, when I pose this "What if ...?" to a youngster, they say, "I would forgive them." (Part of this positive response, of course, is the therapist's perception of the child's readiness for the question.)

Interpret the response: The next step is to interpret the response back to the youngster.

> *Tracy, you've said that if your stepdad came to you and honestly and sincerely apologized to you and asked for your forgiveness, you would forgive him. Is that correct? That means, Tracy, while we were discussing it, you've done YOUR part of the forgiveness. You have made that decision, an important decision that will help you more in the future than you can realize right now. Whether he ever actually asks for your forgiveness or not, you have done your part of the work. That means, Tracy, you don't have to keep dragging a lot of bad baggage around with you. It's like you cut it free, Tracy.*

On occasion, I have encouraged a youngster to compose a "What if ... ?" forgiveness letter. It's perfectly fine (even recommended) for the child or teen to explain once more the depth of hurt and pain they have experienced, the essence of what they are forgiving. The youngster, in the presence of supportive adults and peers, then reads the letter aloud before ceremonially burning it.

This is the spirit of forgiveness. And, like I said, it is powerful and effective stuff.

Acceptance

It would be grossly inappropriate for me to suggest to a youngster she *must* forgive everything. This was brought to my attention when a participant at a seminar shared from her personal experiences how some injustices can be too painful and too troubling to forgive. She understood perfectly the rationale behind the spirit of forgiveness, but suggested acceptance as being the closest to what she could personally achieve.

That made sense to me. Is acceptance enough? It is if, as a result of acceptance and time for it to work, an offended person's life goes back into balance. That would be the best test available, I believe.

What Needs to Happen?

At some point in counseling or therapy, unforgiveness must be addressed if it is the issue that holds back healing. Sensitivity to this point is critical, as it could represent an opportunity for remarkable, positive change and progress.

Work through to forgiveness: I mentioned earlier how, in some cases (such as the death of a person), actual forgiveness is not possible. This could be the case with a youngster who has been the offender.

I had such a patient once, a young man whose drug use had created a strain on his mother. She dies while he was active in his addiction.

His guilt was pressing him into hopelessness. As he went through treatment and worked earnestly on sobriety and recovery, he realized his biggest and most painful regret: the effects of his addition and drug-laden behavior on his mother. We set up an empty chair in group therapy and provided him an opportunity to visit with her one last time about what was on his heart. With support from his counselor and the group, this young man worked through to the forgiveness he so desperately needed from his mother.

That was many years ago. He is doing quite well today.

Guard against misuse: Although the use of the spirit of forgiveness is a powerful boost toward healing, be sensitive to the fact that misuse of it can *deepen* hurt. The process of forgiveness, actual or in spirit, requires the revisiting of painful issues that have been plastered over with layers of anger and rage. If we attempt to remove the anger too quickly, pain can resurface in powerful and destructive ways.

Anger is awesome emotional insulation; it runs on one's desire for happiness. (Think about that for a moment and see if it's not true.) Peeling anger away exposes, one more time, the parts and pieces of the hurt that are to be forgiven. This is a necessary process if forgiveness is to be more than an empty, pointless charade. It is a challenging, but vastly rewarding, experience.

Chapter Twenty-five

Keep Asking "What Needs to Happen?"

Part of the uniqueness of this book is the question that concludes each chapter: "What needs to happen?" We can add insights and strategies to our intervention toolbox but, at some point, we must test them in the *real* world.

And that can be scary, sometimes.

Building Bridges

There's not a parent or teacher alive who hasn't been disappointed in the way they handled a conflict with a child or student. Getting better means learning from those mistakes and getting our hands dirty as we repair weakened or broken bridges of relationships, make them stronger, and build new ones.

But it's not as scary as it might seem. Our children will help us, if we give them the opportunity. In fact, they *want* to help us. They have as much to gain as we do.

Let them help; show them how. You'll be amazed at the results.

Mistakes are Turning Points

We all make mistakes; it's part of the human condition. It's certainly true in the way we address the behavior of young people. We *will* make them, and we generally stand to benefit from them, one way or the other, in the long-run. That's the growth we seek.

The Bible tells of two disciples of Jesus that made life-changing mistakes. The outcomes of those mistakes could not have been more different.

According to the New Testament gospels Judas betrayed Jesus, then later hanged himself. He became bitter in his guilt, too bitter to live. He was certain his act was beyond any forgiveness.

There's not much argument Judas faced a difficult forgiveness issue. That said, here's what I believe: The *only* thing that stood between Judas and forgiveness was Judas.

Peter, fearing for his life, repeatedly denied he even knew Jesus. Yet, with that troubling mistake in his past, Peter became the rock that fit his name, a deeply respected leader of the faith. How did he accomplish that? He owned up to his mistake and vowed he would *never* repeat it, and he didn't. On the Day of Pentecost, Peter stood up and spoke boldly. The power of faith and resolve had replaced fear and doubt.

Peter's mistake jump-started him into becoming better. He did it by not excusing his mistake, but by learning from it. Peter was a fisherman, but he was also good at fixing bridges.

Bitter or better? It's always a choice, isn't it?

"Next Time"

It pays to reflect on what we will do differently "next time," a plan for how we will act to solve a problem or alter an unpleasant outcome in a future opportunity. If we can't learn or won't learn from our experiences, we are shutting the door on a great teacher.

As I mentioned back in Chapter Three, I learned this idea of "next time" from a master back in the late seventies, Dr. William Glasser. I was in Dallas taking his training in Reality Therapy. At that time, Dr. Glasser was doing the training personally. The one mantra he pounded into my head that weekend was "next time."

Dr. Glasser also taught me that many contemporary approaches to discipline don't have a "next time" quality in them. They simply focus on imposing a consequence on behavior. This leaves youngsters to figure out for themselves the cost of inappropriate behavior and how to resolve it. Some can do this, but many cannot. For them, "next time" needs to be an important part of the intervention.

Dr. Glasser made it very clear to me that we cannot reverse a child back through an act of inappropriate behavior, but we can help the youngster develop a better plan for how he will respond to the same circumstances "next time."

"Next time" provides us all yet another opportunity to become even better.

Coffee, G., *Beyond survival: building on the hard times, a pow's inspiring story.* New York: G. P. Putnam's Sons, 1990.

Glasser, W., *Reality therapy: a new approach to psychiatry.* New York: HarperCollins, 1965 (reissued 1989).

Gordon, T., *Parent effectiveness training: the proven program for raising responsible children.* New York: Three Rivers Press, 1970 (revised 2000).

Greene, R., *Lost at school: why our kids with behavioral challenges are falling through the cracks and how we can help them.* New York: Scribners, 2008.

Green, R., *The explosive child: a new approach for understanding and parenting easily frustrated, "chronically inflexible" children.* HarperCollins, 1998.

Hillenbrand, L., *Seabiscuit an american legend.* New York: Random House Publishing Group, 2001.

Kalman, I., "Anger Control Made Easy." A seminar sponsored by Cross Country Education. San Antonio, TX: September, 22, 2004.

Lindbergh, A., *Hour of gold, hour of lead.* New York: Harcourt Brace Jovanovich, 1973, p.213.

Marshall, M., *Parenting without stress: how to raise responsible kids while keeping a life of your own.* Las Alamitas, CA: Piper Press, 2010.

_____, "Promoting Responsibility and Learning." Email newsletter #74 (www.marvinmarshall.com). September 8, 2007.

_____, *Discipline without stress, punishment or rewards.* Las Alamitas, CA: Piper Press, 2001.

Memphis belle, motion picture directed by Michael Caton-Jones. Burbank, CA: Warner Brothers, 1990.

Mr. holland's opus, motion picture directed by Stephen Herek. Burbank, CA: Hollywood Pictures, 1995.

Music of the heart, motion picture directed by Wes Craven. Burbank, CA: Buena Vista, 1999.

Patterson, G., *Coercive family process* (social learning approach, vol 3). Eugene, OR: Castalia Publishing Company, 1982.

Riley, D., *The defiant child: a parent's guide to oppositional defiant disorder.* Dallas, TX: Taylor Publishing Company, 1997.

Ron clark story (the), television movie drama directed by Randa Haines. Atlanta, GA: TNT Television, 2006.

Shapiro, J., "Therapy for Tough Kids and Their Beleaguered Families." A seminar sponsored by Cross Country Education. San Antonio, TX, September 9, 2005.

Stand and deliver, Motion picture directed by Ramon Menendez. Burbank, CA: Warner Brothers, 1988

Sutton, J., *What parents need to know about odd: up-to-date insights and ideas for managing oppositional defiant disorder and other defiant behaviors.* Pleasanton, TX: Friendly Oaks Publications, 2007.

————, *60 Ways to reach a difficult and defiant child: a guide for counselors.* Pleasanton, TX: Friendly Oaks Publications, 2007.

————, *101 Ways to make your classroom special: creating a place where significance, teamwork and spontaneity can sprout and flourish.* Pleasanton, TX: Friendly Oaks Publications, 1999.

————, *If my kid's so nice ... why's he driving me crazy? straight talk about the "good kid" disorder.* Pleasanton, TX: Friendly Oaks Publications, 1997.

Vitale., J., Hew Len, I., *Zero limits: the secret hawaiian system for wealth, health, peace, and more*. Hoboken, NJ: John Wiley & Sons, 2007.

Wenger, W., Poe, R., *The einstein factor: a proven method for increasing your intelligence*. New York: Prima Lifestyles, 1995.

Wenning, K., *Winning cooperation from your child: a comprehensive method to stop defiant and aggressive behavior in children* (revised). Northvale, NJ: Jason Aronson, 1999.

Wenning, K., Nathan, P., King, S. "Mood disorders in children with oppositional defiant disorder: a pilot study." *American journal of orthopsychiatry*, 1993; 63(2): 295-299.

About the Author: James Sutton started out working for the government, the United States Navy. As a member of the Naval Security Group, he saw combat duty in Vietnam with the Third Marine Amphibious Force in the late 1960s. He earned his college degree and teaching certificate as a GI-Bill student, and then taught learning and emotionally-challenged youngsters as a Special Education teacher while he earned his master's degree in school psychology.

It was as a school psychologist that Jim developed exceptional skills in assessing and outlining management and treatment for emotionally and behaviorally troubled youngsters. Demand for these skills grew when he completed his doctorate, earned his license as a psychologist, opened a private practice, and began consulting, writing, speaking, and training nationally. His clients have included universities (over four dozen of them), schools and school districts, residential treatment centers, group and foster homes, hospitals, juvenile justice authorities, drug and alcohol treatment facilities, and child-service agencies.

In addition to *The Changing Behavior Book*, Jim has written other books, including *If My Kid's So Nice ... Why's He Driving ME Crazy? 101 Ways to Make Your Classroom Special, What Parents Need to Know About ODD*, and *60 Ways to Reach a Difficult and Defiant Child*. He is a contributor to the award-winning parent blog, www.EmpoweringParents.com, and he edits his own monthly email publication, the *ODD Management Digest* (available at no cost through his website).

For information regarding consultation or training, go to his website at www.DocSpeak.com, or call (800) 659-6628 toll free.

Index

_____

To Purchase Another Copy
of This Book

Call (830) 569-3586, or go to

www.thechangingbehaviorbook.com

Notes:

CPSIA information can be obtaine
Printed in the USA
LVOW061926150911

246433LV00003B/2/P

31901052066851

9 781878 878779